MONOPOLY

THE STORY BEHIND
THE WORLD'S BEST-SELLING GAME

LANTIC
VENUE

E $260

PENNSYLVANIA RAILROAD

PRICE $200

ILLI
AVE

PRICE

MONOPOLY®
BRAND

THE STORY BEHIND THE WORLD'S BEST-SELLING GAME

By Rod Kennedy, Jr.

Text by Jim Waltzer

In Association with
The Atlantic City Historical Museum

Gibbs Smith, Publisher
Salt Lake City

First Edition
08 07 06 05 04   5 4 3 2 1

Published by
Gibbs Smith, Publisher
P. O. Box 667
Layton, UT 84041

www.gibbs-smith.com
orders: 1.800.748.5439

Designed by Linda Herman
Printed in Hong Kong

Library of Congress Cataloging-in-Publication Data

Kennedy, Rod, 1944-
  Monopoly, the story behind the world's best-selling game / by Rod Kennedy,
Jr.; text by Jim Waltzer in association with The Atlantic City Historical
Museum.—1st ed.
    p. cm.
  ISBN 1-58685-322-8
  1. Monopoly (Game)—History 2. Atlantic City (N.J.)—History. I. Title.
GV1469.M65K46 2004
794—dc22
                        2004013643

Contents

CHANCE

DEDICATION

To Vicki Gold Levi,
My friend and colleague, sometimes Jewish mother,
and one of Atlantic City's all-time greatest boosters.

ACKNOWLEDGMENTS

A book like this would not have been possible without the help and cooperation of many others, and I wish to thank the following individuals and institutions who helped me to make this dream a reality:
Vicki Gold Levi for everything. Jim Waltzer for capturing the vision. Gibbs Smith and Christopher Robbins for saying yes. Tom Klusaritz and Joshua Izzo for permission. Allen "Boo" Pergament, Anthony J. Kutschera, and Joseph and John Palillo for Atlantic City. Lindy Davis, Vesa Nelson, and Marc Sullivan for Henry George. Robert E. Ruffalo Jr. and Herbert B. Stern for the museum association. Ron Lieberman for his good eye. The Metropolitan Post Card Collectors Club, Mary L. Martin, LTD. Postcards, and all the dealers and sources for the images.

MONOPOLY:

The Story Behind the World's Best-Selling Game combines two of my favorite things—MONOPOLY and Atlantic City. Some of my fondest childhood memories are of long, drawn-out MONOPOLY games on rainy Saturday or Sunday afternoons with family and friends—and it is more than just a childhood memory. MONOPOLY is a game I have enjoyed playing throughout my life. It was even the basis of a relationship that started out as a MONOPOLY challenge in a bar one night. In fact, I love the game so much that my home would not be complete without a MONOPOLY set in the closet.

Like most people, I once thought that the colored properties on the classic MONOPOLY game board were fictional places that existed only as I imagined them, so it was one of the great discoveries in my life to learn that they really do exist in a place called Atlantic City.

My first trip to Atlantic City was in the summer of 1973. I was thrilled to be really taking a walk on the Boardwalk and advancing to St. Charles Place. I was captivated by the ornate and elegant hotels looking like giant sandcastles built along a Boardwalk lined with shops, restaurants, and giant amusement piers jutting into the sea. And even though this once thriving and fashionable resort known as "the Queen of Resorts" and "America's Playground" was in decline, I still sensed the ghosts of years gone by and was possessed. The deal was

further sealed when I learned that my parents had honeymooned in Atlantic City, and that I was most probably conceived in the Shelbourne Hotel.

Several years later, I was invited by "America's Best Loved Photographer," Bud Lee, and Susan Dintenfass Subtle to join them in a photo shoot of the diving-horse lady on Steel Pier. It was from this experience that Susan and I conceived of the idea to do a nostalgic book about Atlantic City, which eventually was so wonderfully brought to fruition by Vicki Gold Levi and Lee Eisenberg, and called *Atlantic City: 125 Years of Ocean Madness*. The book, which takes a long and loving look at Atlantic City as The Capitol of Americana, was published in 1979, and has gone through many subsequent printings and is still in print today.

While *Atlantic City: 125 Years of Ocean Madness* touched briefly upon the connection between Atlantic City and MONOPOLY, I still wanted to do a book that would be a visualization of the classic MONOPOLY game board illustrated with Atlantic City images that would bring to life for the very first time the very real place upon which this game, enjoyed for generations by millions of people around the world, was based. Now, thanks to Gibbs Smith, Publisher, and Hasbro, I am able to do so in this volume.

—Rod Kennedy, Jr., New York City

The Game—A Brief History of MONOPOLY

The third time was a charm.

Twice the executives at Parker Brothers in Salem, Massachusetts, turned down this table game about money and real estate. The second version, submitted by one Charles B. Darrow, was deemed too complicated. The year was 1934, the Great Depression was under way, and the enterprising Philadelphian wanted America's premier game maker to market his handmade creation. Undaunted by the rejection, he took the next step on his own, printing copies and selling them through local department stores and the New York–based toy company, FAO Schwarz.

Luckily, for the overextended Darrow, his game was a hit. When word reached Parker Brothers, the firm reconsidered its earlier appraisal and licensed Darrow's game—it was called MONOPOLY. In 1935, it became the best-selling board game in America. In the seven decades since, more than 750 million sets have been sold and MONOPOLY has gained a world-wide audience. It is played by kid capitalists and adult dreamers on kitchen tables and patio decks, in living rooms and in basements. It rescued Parker Brothers from the doldrums of the Great Depression and made Darrow a rich man.

But before all of that, the first move belonged to a woman named Lizzie.

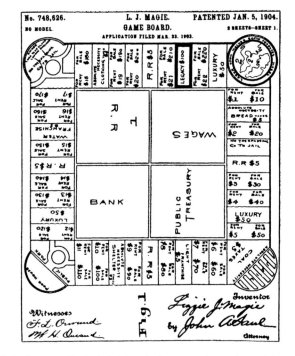

Left: Free spirit Elizabeth J. Magie had a passion for equality and the economic teachings of Henry George. Her table game, first patented in 1904, was the ancestor of MONOPOLY, but the mass-marketed game evolved from socially conscious Georgist doctrine to two-fisted capitalism. Here is Lizzie later in life (with her middle/maiden name misspelled) after she had married Albert Phillips and sold her patent.

Above: The original game board as patented by Lizzie Magie in 1904 offered generic real estate for sale or rent and the benevolent starting point, "Mother Earth" (upper right-hand square). A railroad centered on each of the four linear pathways, water and electric utilities, a luxury tax, and the ominous command "Go to Jail" anticipated the future game of MONOPOLY.

Long before the familiar layout of Chance and Community Chest and color-coded Atlantic City Avenues, there was a creative young woman who believed in her Quaker teachings and the power of economics. In 1904, Elizabeth J. Magie, fledgling game inventor from Virginia, patented a forty-space game board that included railroads, utilities, and the treacherous corner "Go to Jail." She called her game "The Landlord's Game." Rents were collected on real estate of increasing value, the properties were name-less, and contestants traveled clockwise along the board's square pathway—truly a rudimentary version of the iconic American game called MONOPOLY.

Charles Darrow, the game's reputed creator—a man whose name and image grace a plaque on the Atlantic City Boardwalk—showed up three decades later. And though he didn't invent the game out of whole cloth, he did transform it into a mass-merchandising home run. He recognized the game's commercial potential and took the steps to realize it. Darrow had the vision and, as it turned out, Parker Brothers supplied the marketing muscle.

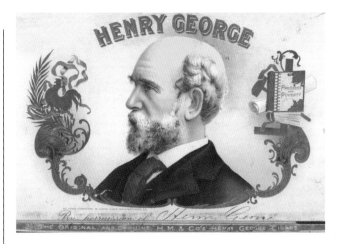

In his lifetime, many people thought Henry George (here on a cigar box cover) was blowing smoke, but just as many deemed him the sage of the century. His book *Progress and Poverty*, published in 1880, decried the unequal distribution of wealth in the U.S. and argued that a "single tax" (on real estate) replacing all others in the tax code would create balance and chase away poverty. While his plan was never enacted, his personality impressed the public—George became almost as recognizable as Mark Twain. His socioeconomic philosophy inspired Elizabeth Magie to devise a table game that evolved into a celebration of all that he opposed.

Though not intended as such, this Georgian graphic, with its houses and properties, bears a striking resemblance to the MONOPOLY board.

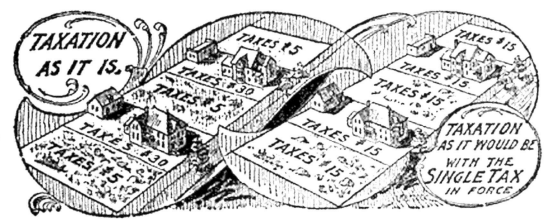

9

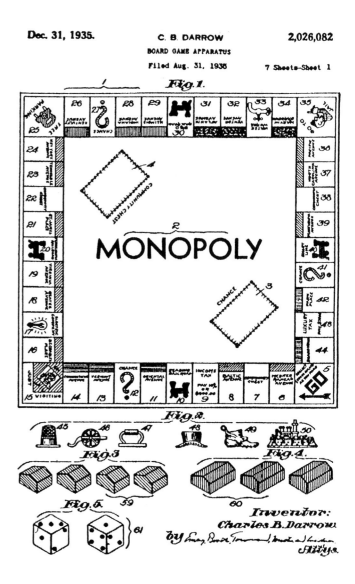

Above: Early box cover.

Right: After piecing together several sets by hand and being rebuffed by Parker Brothers in 1934, Charles Darrow enlisted the services of a printer to produce a greater volume of games and sold them in local stores and at FAO Schwarz in New York. In addition to a promotional flair, he had an eye for graphics. His added design features turned a rather plain game board into an American icon. Chance and Community Chest cards were reshaped from square to a sleeker rectangular. Property squares received color bars, and a variety of colors throughout spiced the previously drab board. The Chance square sprouted a large question mark, the GO square big bold letters and an arrow. Quirky characters and symbols popped up all across the board: the "prisoner" behind jail bars, the pointing policeman who sent him there, the choo-choo at the railroad crossings, the plump car at Free Parking, the ready faucet at Water Works, and the light bulb on the electric utility square.

LIZZIE'S JOURNEY

It is likely that soon after launching her game, Magie joined the liberal movement inspired by economist-lecturer Henry George, whose *Progress and Poverty*, published a quarter-century earlier, held that all taxes be abolished except for that on real estate and, in general, argued for a redistribution of wealth. The Philadelphia-born George declaimed that "land is a gift of nature" and all men have an equal right to its use. The value of land, he said, stemmed from our collective economic activity. He wanted government to tax the underlying land but not the improvements on it, insisting that if the tax were then gradually increased, the landowner would have further incentive to make his property more productive and offset the higher tax bill.

George was a popular figure in his day, and many found his theories logical and appealing. An experimental community in Arden, Delaware, was noteworthy for adopting Georgist doctrine. As early as 1910, some of the Arden "single taxers" were playing Lizzie Magie's real estate game, and one of them introduced it to his brother, University of Pennsylvania Wharton School Professor Scott Nearing, a socialist economist who saw evil embedded in capitalism.

The game migrated to other college campuses, towns, and cities. Magie sold copies but did not enforce her patent. Her game traveled on homemade boards of wood, linen, and cardboard, with the players taking the liberty to modify the rules and change the names of properties to those of local streets and avenues. If single taxers were playing to point out the moral flaws of capitalism, others, like students in their dorms or homeowners in their drawing rooms, were reveling in the simulation of moneymaking and ruthless business tactics. The most telling of the new rules organized properties into groups and assigned higher rents to a given group owned by one player.

Money Man: Philadelphian Charles B. Darrow lay claim to inventing MONOPOLY and affectionately naming the game's streets after those of his favorite vacation destination, Atlantic City. Darrow grasped the game's potential and had the drive to take it to the top. In true MONOPOLY fashion, he capitalized on its underlying popularity.

Properties could then be improved to yield even greater income. With its status as a "folk" game increasing, Magie's diversion began to be called the "monopoly" game.

In 1924—two full decades after obtaining her first patent for The Landlord's Game—the now married Elizabeth Magie Phillips secured a second patent and incorporated many of the play-action changes made by herself and others. With its Chicago cachet (the Loop and Lake Shore Drive were stops along the board), The Landlord Game reflected Phillips' relocation to Illinois, and in this version she tailored the rules so that the abuses of landowning were underscored—no longer was the goal to bankrupt the opposition but to rescue "poor" players and create level economic footing. In the intervening years, Phillips had become headmistress of the Henry George School of Social Science, and her allegiance was clearly to the late pundit's conception of an unfair landlord system. Seeking not wealth but the education of the public, she contacted Parker Brothers' founder, George Parker. Her bid was declined.

As Phillips tried to promote her revised game, the folk game of monopoly continued to grow in popularity. In the late

1920s, two Delta Kappa Epsilon and real-life brothers, Frederick and Louis Thun, recruited one Daniel W. Layman into the monopoly-playing fraternity at Williams College in Reading, Pennsylvania. When he returned to his hometown of Indianapolis, Layman found fresh converts. He eventually drew up formal rules, made an Indianapolis-flavored board, and marketed his game under the name "Finance." But by then, the monopoly game had shifted back East and taken on a decidedly seashore profile.

One of the Indianapolis newcomers in the Layman pipeline was a woman named Ruth Hoskins, who moved to Atlantic City and became a teacher at the local Friends School in October 1929, just as

Above: This MONOPOLY set made by Charles Darrow circa 1933 is the earliest of his sets known to exist. Darrow fashioned a circular game board and created the other elements by hand, coloring the oilcloth, typing deeds and cards, and cutting "houses" and "hotels" from wood molding. He produced one to two sets per day by this method, and soon found himself unable to keep up with demand. He then hired a printer, who increased production to six sets daily. The Forbes Collection, New York. **Left:** Darrow eventually changed his homemade MONOPOLY game board from a circle to a square, a shape that seemed better suited to the sharp movements of financial wheeler-dealers. The Forbes Collection, New York.

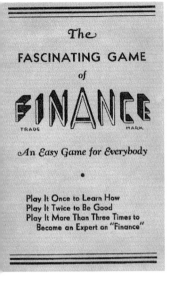

Wall Street was about to crash and usher in the Great Depression. But this roving game of monopoly would soon enter an explosive bull market. Hoskins and her Quaker acquaintances refined the rules and changed the map to utilize Atlantic City street names, many pegged to the residences of the players in Hoskins' circle, thus etching themselves into the game's landscape. Two of the regular Atlantic City players indoctrinated Charles E. Todd in the mysterious ways of monopoly. Todd, a hotelier from the Germantown section of Philadelphia, was a longtime friend of Charles Brace Darrow's wife. At the time, Darrow was an unemployed heating salesman who lived in the area and soon made the monopoly game a pastime.

Darrow sensed the potential in the game on the oilcloth and asked Todd to provide him with written rules and a copy of the game board. Darrow felt he had stumbled across a product with commercial potential and obtained a copyright in 1933 for this Atlantic City version, which he transformed from a rather drab-looking game to the graphic icon we know and love today. The next year, he brought his new game of MONOPOLY—with a capital M—to Parker Brothers, who flinched at its complexity and rejected it. A determined Darrow borrowed money so he could produce copies and sell them in Philadelphia and New York. His instincts were correct: the game was as much of a hit with the public as it had been when circulated by private hands in the East and Midwest.

One day, an FAO Schwarz shopper purchased the game and was sufficiently impressed to recommend it to a friend, who happened to be the wife of Parker Brothers' president, Robert Barton. When Barton's fifty-year-old firm then learned of Darrow's preliminary success, it finally recognized the game's commercial appeal. Parker Brothers struck an agreement with Darrow and patented MONOPOLY in 1935. Now, with genuine marketing and production power behind it, the game took off, with sales reaching 200,000 in a month.

Darrow was on his way to riches and Parker Brothers had a timely meal ticket. However, there was some unfinished business. The latest patent conflicted with the earlier Lizzie Magie Phillips patents, and

A very early FAO Schwarz ad, probably before 1936.
Above, left: Daniel W. Layman's adaptation of the folk game of monopoly in the late 1920s was more concerned with high finance than in curing society's ills. He learned the game at college, then developed his own version.

MONOPOLY resembled both The Landlord's Game and the game of Finance, which creator Daniel Layman had sold to a small games manufacturer. Parker Brothers purchased both the rights to Finance and the Magie Phillips patents. Lizzie still prized loyalty more than royalties; she wanted only to spread the Gospel by George, and hoped that her revised second game would now find wider audiences.

MONOPOLY had a new landlord, and Charles Darrow was in the penthouse. A grassroots game whose most passionate fans sought to share the wealth was now claimed by a sole creator and produced by the king of the gamemakers. Its "playing" goal of achieving wealth and squelching the competition mirrored the rough-and-ready settlement of America and seemed to capture the yearnings of a Depression-era population.

The Place—A Brief History of Atlantic City

Like many cities across the country, Atlantic City grew out of an economic monopoly or, actually, a series of monopolies, reminding us of a certain board game in which players try to buy up all of the properties and reap the financial reward. Atlantic City, whose streets make up the properties on the classic MONOPOLY game board, was a grand seashore resort designed for the common man, but its business plan entailed profits for the privileged few.

Simply put, that was the American way. Though the nation had been born in a revolt against foreign monarchial rule, the new expanding country created its own aristocracy of landowners. In those days preceding income taxes, government financed itself principally through trade tariffs and the sale of land, and before the populace had an opportunity to buy small

parcels, frontline speculators had first crack. Typically, they acquired large chunks on the cheap and split them into little pieces to be resold at a tidy profit. This is the time-honored art of "land booming."

The engine of America's westward (in the case of Atlantic City, eastward) expansion was the railroads, which acquired land for free or at a deep discount from a government intent on spreading settlers coast to coast. The government was offering not only the right-of-way to lay track, but also sizable stretches of adjacent land for settlement. The railroads,

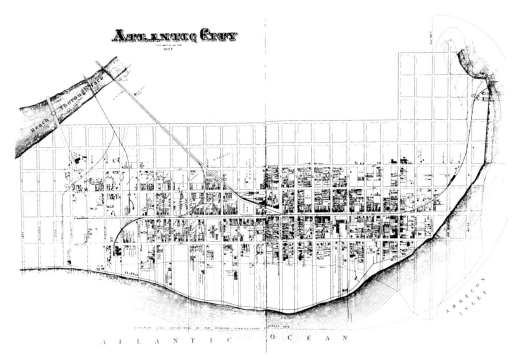

Atlantic City Map 1877— The avenues paralleling beach and ocean took the names of the world's great seas, while the verticals were named after the states in the Union.

Above: He came riding into town looking like Ichabod Crane, but Dr. Jonathan Pitney wasn't spooked by Absecon Island. The lanky M.D. envisioned the sparsely populated seaside as a grand resort and convinced the public (and maybe himself) that the sand and salt air had curative powers. Beyond the hype, he was a trusted doctor and a tireless advocate of growth and improvement in the region. History pegs him as the Father of Atlantic City, and his inland home is a guesthouse a century-and-a-half later.

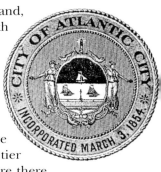

A section of the state of New Jersey official document incorporating the Camden and Atlantic Railroad Company, the business entity that launched Atlantic City and several personal fortunes. The state act authorized the new company to convey land, issue stock, and transact other business as "necessary or expedient."

Above, right: With Richard B. Osborne's classic name on the seal, the newly incorporated city went into the books on March 3, 1854.

Opposite, top: Philadelphia engineer Richard B. Osborne girded Dr. Pitney's vision with technical expertise, convincing the construction industry that a city could be built on sand and drawing up a master plan for Atlantic City's development. In addition, Osborne coined the name "Atlantic City," mapped out the street grid, and helped name the streets after the states in the Union.

in effect, built cities on that land, where value skyrocketed with access.

The dynamic of land settlement in the future United States of America dates to the early years of the Colonial age when the crowned heads of Europe began to sense the frontier across the ocean. Long before there were barnacled piers and flashy casinos in Atlantic City, for example, the land was as tightly held as a pot-winning hand of poker. A dozen Englishmen led by William Penn owned all of New Jersey in the late seventeenth century before selling 15,000 acres (at four cents per acre) on either side of the Great Egg Harbor River to Quaker farmer Thomas Budd. This amalgam of marshes and dunes that was to become Atlantic City was situated on Absecon Island, the name derived from the Lenape Indians' Absegami, or "Little Sea Water."

Budd didn't live on it but anted up for the island acreage because the colonizers made it a requirement for acquiring more desirable real estate inland. The first actual island dweller didn't appear on the scene for another 160 years, and by 1850, only a half-dozen other intrepid families had joined him among the cedars and bramble, the mosquitoes and blacksnakes. When the elements lashed them, the islanders received medical treatment from physician Jonathan Pitney, who came by horseback from the mainland village of Absecon.

Pitney had arrived in South Jersey thirty years earlier and was an M.D. with an eye for business and politics. A considerable landowner (500 acres' worth), he'd been a county freeholder, state constitutional convention delegate, and Congressional candidate. Now in his early fifties, he was about to give life to his Big Idea, one he'd been incubating for decades. Convinced that sand and sea were good for what ails the human body, he envisioned a railroad linking city folk to the healthful climes of the beach, and a resort rising on Absecon Island like a storm-swelled wave. Making money, felt the good doctor, was not an unhealthful activity.

The city slickers he had in mind, of course, would come from Philadelphia, fifty miles due west. The new vacation haven would be, in medical and metaphorical parlance, "Philadelphia's lungs." And in Philadelphia engineer Richard Osborne, Pitney found a spiritual partner with technical expertise. Having participated in the mushrooming of the city of Chicago, Osborne had brought his boomtown mentality east. Sending a railroad across marshland and building a city on sand were not simple matters, but Osborne had persuasive answers for a coterie of capitalists assembled by Pitney, mostly glass manufacturers from South Jersey towns.

Meanwhile, the doctor-developer extolled the health benefits of the seashore and stoked his connections in state government. In 1852, the legislature chartered the Camden and Atlantic Railroad, and Pitney's People gobbled up the tendered shares. The railroad proceeded to buy land hand-over-fist on the skinny, ten-mile-long island until the legislature halted the frenzy. The beach barons skirted that obstacle by forming the Camden and Atlantic Land Company,

The railroads realized that visitors transported to Atlantic City needed a place to stay, and "excursion" houses at the end of the line were the logical answer. They were convenient for train travelers and extended the land developers' business monopoly. Celebrities were particularly sought to give early Atlantic City a cachet, and so railroaders, the "cottage" community, and store merchants joined forces to attract them. Inducements included a free trip by train, carriages and yachts for luxurious transport, and "entertainment." Snare a president or two, and your new resort was immediately on the map. Better yet, recruit physician-guests and they'd be favorably disposed to sing the praises of a healthful climate and the ocean's healing properties. That the ocean could also be treacherous at times was evident in the surf in front of the New Excursion House in 1868 Atlantic City. Cables extended from beach masts to ocean anchors, and lifelines hung like laundry at nine-foot intervals. The apparatus was patented by one Captain William Tell Street, whose name befit his aim.

THE SOUVENIR CHROMO

Seaside House

Greeting from ATLANTIC CITY, N.J.

COPYRIGHT 1895 BY C.VOELKER.

The very first Atlantic City postcard superimposed the sporty Seaside House built on a curving boardwalk (the presence of a railing suggests Boardwalk number four, completed 1889) with the receded lighthouse (completed 1857) in the distance.

and resumed their land grab. Average purchase prices of $10 per acre increased up to thirty-fold after the railroad was completed.

If they had been playing MONOPOLY, Pitney and company would already have been winners. The railroad and the land company were like meshing gears, each improving the other's bottom line. The prime investors added one more cog to the machine by building a large "excursion house" at the end of the line for easy drop-off of passengers . . . and still more profits. From the Philadelphia-Camden waterfront to the sandy doorstep of the Atlantic Ocean, this ambitious enterprise had all the earmarks of, yes, a monopoly.

What it also had, undeniably, was momentum. In late 1853, Osborne unfurled his final survey map for the railroad directors, and there, stretched in large letters across an artist's rendition of ocean waves, was the name proposed for the new resort. An inspired name, straightforward yet poetic. ATLANTIC CITY.

Either Osborne or one of the directors (or both) fashioned names to fill out the map's grid, linking the north-south avenues to the great seas (Pacific, Atlantic, Arctic, Baltic, Mediterranean) and the east-west streets to the states of the Union, a union that would threaten to unravel within a decade. But such a thought was unthinkable when the Pitney-Osborne team fleshed out its creation.

Names carried a certain weight, and the city founders reached high for symbolism. From its very genesis, Atlantic City—soon to be dubbed Queen of America's Resorts—had a national profile. In March 1854, the state of New Jersey granted Atlantic City a municipal charter and, four months later, the first train chugged into town atop the newly laid rails. Reporters poured out of the cars, were ferried across the bay, and hoofed it to the excursion house. The word was out, and soon hostelries and cottages appeared like clamshells ushered in by the tide.

Below: The Camden and Atlantic Railroad was the artery that pumped vacationing Philadelphians to the novel seashore resort Atlantic City, cutting a swath through the South Jersey hinterlands all the way to the beach. Eastbound trains departed from a Camden station that received ferries from Philadelphia's Vine Street wharf across the Delaware River.

UNITED STATES HOTEL, ATLANTIC CITY, N.J. PROP'S. & OWNERS, BROWN & WOELPPER.

COLLECTION OF J. E. KRANEFELD

MAP: CIRCA 1877

Above: Built in 1854 by the Camden and Atlantic Railroad as the lodging in the brand new resort, the United States Hotel was the first of the grandiose Atlantic City hotels. Its six hundred rooms made it the largest in the nation at the time. Located between Delaware and Maryland Avenues, the property at one time stretched two city blocks from Atlantic Avenue to the beach, and management ushered guests to beach bathhouses via a mule-drawn tram on tracks. An 1890s infestation of mosquitoes so unsettled this place, where battle-tested U. S. Grant and other American presidents regularly stayed, that it never recovered. In the new century, United States Avenue (between Delaware and Maryland) was shortened to States Avenue and widened into the broadest, most beautiful boulevard in the city.

ATLANTIC CITY'S original business plan was predicated on drawing vacationers from Philadelphia in the pre-auto era. There was only one means of transportation that could bring the masses overland to the seashore: rail travel.

The Camden and Atlantic Railroad received its charter two years before Atlantic City was incorporated, and when the new line began whisking summer-parched Philadelphians by the carload to the emerging Shangri-la-by-the-sea, the beach became a bonanza. The Railroad gave rise to the Camden and Atlantic Land Company, as real estate values spiked and a monopolistic few practiced the unsubtle art of town-booming.

As the city added hotels and mule-drawn streetcars and civic institutions, competition colored rail travel, but not too much. Two Camden and Atlantic directors left the pioneer line in 1876 to launch the Narrow-Gauge, which was absorbed by the Philadelphia and Reading Railroad seven years later and changed to standard-gauge. That same year, the mighty Pennsylvania Railroad, which had already connected New York to Atlantic City, bought the Camden and Atlantic. Thirty years after the concept of the city by the sea had germinated, the original moneymen or their heirs were reaping multiple fortunes.

A century later, declining passenger rail travel in the United States roughly paralleled Atlantic City's retreat from the peak, as airplanes flew vacationers to Florida and Vegas, and cars made closer options available.

If the railroads fueled Atlantic City's explosive growth, in the game of MONOPOLY they are stable revenue producers. With one situated on each of the four game board pathways, and rents doubling with each additional property purchased, they provide what investors expect of big-ticket assets: steady income. On the MONOPOLY tracks, the Reading and the Pennsylvania railroads reflect authentic seashore history, but the B & O (Baltimore and Ohio) was primarily a freight line and never stopped in Atlantic City. And as you'll see on page 23, there was no Short Line at all.

The Philadelphia and Reading Railroad's seashore run catered to a ridership of modest means. In time, the company dropped the Philadelphia portion of its name and merged with the massive Pennsylvania Railroad, which had swallowed up the original Camden and Atlantic. MONOPOLY kept the two great names as separate properties.

BROAD STREET STATION, PHILADELPHIA, PA.

At the seashore we have landed ;
For a good time we are bound
In the next mail I will tell you
What enjoyment we have foun

Above, left: Opposite City Hall in Philadelphia, Broad Street Station was the Pennsy's hub, and as grandiose as any European cathedral. In the twentieth century, eastbound trains headed for Atlantic City originated or stopped here.

Above, center: In the early days, mosquitoes and sand plagued seashore rail cars, and not all riders were as contented as this couple. But they kept coming to the Victorian resort that spawned decidedly non-Victorian behavior.

Left: The Baltimore and Ohio Railroad laid the first mile of railroad right-of-way in America, but the only stop it ever made in Atlantic City was in the minds of MONOPOLY players.

22

ATLANTIC CITY

A TRIP TO THE SHORE   1

"SHORE FAST LINE"

Electric Service to

OCEAN CITY

PLEASANTVILLE,
NORTHFIELD,
(Golf Course)
LINWOOD,
SOMERS POINT.

ATLANTIC CITY

Virginia Avenue and Boardwalk

TO

OCEAN CITY

Eighth Street and Boardwalk

FREQUENT SERVICE VIA
Atlantic Ave. and Longport Division
TO VENTNOR, MARGATE
AND LONGPORT

60   PENNSYLVANIA-READING SEASHORE LINES, ATLANTIC CITY, N. J.

Above: The Shore Fast Line, formally known as the Atlantic City and Shore Railroad, began sending people from beach to mainland in 1906. Its curtained, open-air trolleys departed from Virginia Avenue and the Boardwalk. The trolleys yielded to buses for all mainland runs from 1948 on. The Short Line R. R. was the MONOPOLY counterpart to the Shore Fast Line.

Left: In 1934, Atlantic City's Union Station at Arkansas and Arctic Avenues became the final stop for the Pennsylvania-Reading Seashore Lines, and a busy bus depot as well. The stately, classical building stood until 2001.

THE PROPERTIES

AS THE FOLK GAME of monopoly traveled across the countryside, the critical route turned out to be Ruth Hoskins's passage from Indianapolis to the New Jersey seashore. There, as a teacher at the Atlantic City Friends School, she recruited some of her colleagues to play the game, and it soon became an evening activity that held their interest and didn't thin their wallets. (This was, after all, during the Depression.)

The new recruits made their own game boards on oilcloth, and after a while they decided to change the game's geography. These Atlantic City Quakers put the enduring stamp of the seashore on MONOP-OLY by giving game board properties the names of local streets that had a direct bearing on their lives. Hoskins and fellow teacher Ruth Harvey lived on Pennsylvania Avenue, so that street became a "property" on Quaker oilcloth. Similarly, other Atlantic City street names worked their way onto the board: Harvey's daughter walked across North Carolina Avenue to get to the Friends School on Pacific Avenue, the nanny of the Harvey household lived on Baltic Avenue, some of the school's more well-to-do students lived in Marven Gardens, a board member owned the Hotel Morton on Virginia Avenue.

Indeed, the fact that a number of Atlantic City's grand hotels were Quaker-owned further influenced the game's evolution. As something of a tribute, Hoskins and her converts, many of whom lived in these hostelries at minimum cost courtesy of the ownership, decided to add "hotels" to a real estate landscape that had been limited to "houses." They also introduced fixed prices for each property, elimi-nating the auction method that they decided was not appropriate for Quakers. A man named Jesse Raiford, who was part of Hoskins's Quaker circle, compiled a balanced list of rents and prices true to the Atlantic City housing market. In time, Raiford would pass the game on to Charles Todd, who would pass it on to Charles Darrow, who would close the deal once and for all.

The Landlord's Game inspired numerous spinoffs. One version became popular in Atlantic City, where the players renamed the avenues after familiar Atlantic City avenues. Charles E. Todd created this MONOPOLY set in 1932 and used it to teach the game to Charles Darrow, who later marketed MONOPOLY as his own invention. The Forbes Collection, New York.

NEW YORK AVENUE

TENNESSEE AVENUE

COMMUNITY CHEST

PRICE $18C

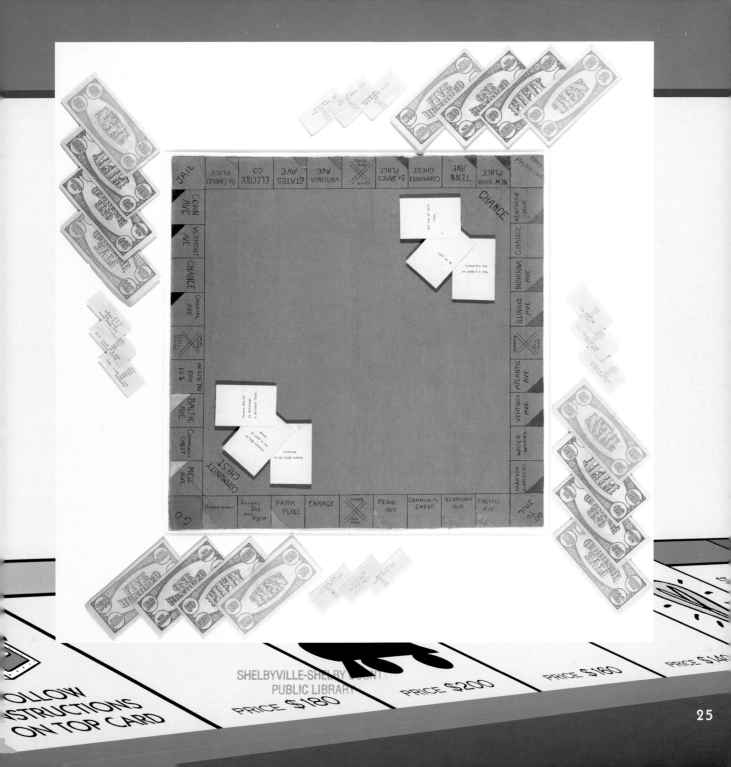

MEDITERRANEAN AVENUE was largely a commercial, light-industrial stretch that featured the likes of Abbotts Dairies and Wrigley's Chewing Gum, and ended with Hackney's seafood restaurant on Absecon Inlet.

Hackney's and nearby Captain Starn's made the inlet synonymous with hearty seafood, but the area was also known for its recreational and commercial activities on the water. Starn's maintained a fleet of sailboats and motorboats that gave sightseers a tour of the island, and a fresh fish market and packing house for anglers' daily harvests.

Back on the avenue, however, there was only the drabness of pavement and wooden boarding houses. The other dark purple property, Baltic Avenue, was known for offering accommodations to African-American visitors and many of the kitchen and house-keeping workers who staffed the hotels near and on the Boardwalk.

Mediterranean and Baltic are the least expensive properties on the MONOPOLY board, and give players a chance to buy on the cheap. Investors must consider, however, that the two properties receive fewer "stops" over the course of a game than any other property group, just as the real-life streets get less traffic than do those closer to the ocean. A statistical ranking based on cost, rents, and frequency of stops by other players places them next to last among the ten property groups. (An opponent's trip around the board returns an average 13.6 cents on each investment dollar made by a landlord who has built a hotel on his dark purple property.) Still, the DPs show relative strength early in the game when the board is largely undeveloped.

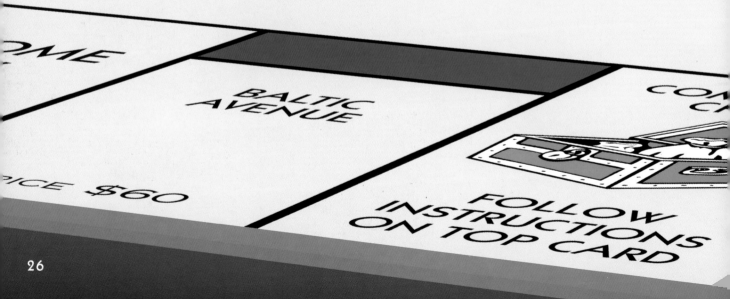

Lobster King Harry Hackney with his Lobster Waitresses who won the Prize in Atlantic City's Famous Beauty Pageant Parade on the Atlantic City Boardwalk

Above: The familiar giant lobster symbolized Hackney's and its vaunted seafood cuisine. Sometimes the waitresses really dressed the part. Situated on Absecon Inlet at Maine and Mediterranean Avenues, Hackney's sat at the confluence of trolleys, jitneys, and hungry seafood patrons. Founded by Harry Hackney in 1912, it fed some 800,000 diners annually in its heyday. One of them was Hackney's friend Al Smith, governor of New York, who remarked that eating at the restaurant was like "fishing out the window," a phrase that stuck. Indeed, a pier in front of the restaurant offered the chance to fish for kingfish, weakfish, flounder, and other tasty species of the Atlantic. Hackney's canned its own brand of seafood products, such as clam chowder, right on the premises, and its "purified lobster pools" attracted spectators who watched a constant stream of ocean-pumped saltwater bathe the crustacean of their choice.

OUR SEA FOODS ARE CAUGHT BY OUR OWN BOATS

CAPT. STARN'S

Sea Food Restaurant and Bar

ATLANTIC CITY N. J.

OUT OF THE WATER INTO THE PAN

Over the Sea Bar

All Kinds of Boating

Capt. Starn — and Crew — That Serves You
Dine at The Captain's Table

Ample Parking Space—Free

Above: Captain Starn's was a sprawling complex that served up boat excursions and yapping sea lions along with seafood platters. The Starn's roster of sailing sloops and Miss Atlantic City speedboats ushered an estimated one million people on sightseeing tours each year. For those seeking greater thrills, a "diving seaplane" with a reversible-pitch propeller descended from the sky and hit the water with a thud. The affectionate sea lions cavorted in their outdoor pens, playing to the crowd. Starn's grew from a one-story dining room to include an adjoining dining hall, the upstairs Captain's Bridge, the outdoor Captain's Mess, the Over-the-Sea Bar (upper left), and the Yacht Bar fashioned from, naturally, a yacht.

Right: Abbotts Dairies was a major part of the Mediterranean Avenue commercial district. In keeping with the health-conscious seashore, the company emphasized its product safety standards.

Right: Prohibition or not, Atlantic City kept the spigot open, and as any stoolie could tell you, the evidence was strong at Weekes' Tavern at Baltic and Illinois. Weekes' began as a liquor store and transformed itself into a cocktail lounge with live entertainment, including a house band. Jazz great Grover Washington and romantic balladeer Arthur Prysock both played here.

Below: Baltic Avenue's Liberty Hotel touted itself as "the most modern and best equipped hotel for colored people in the East," including 141 suites, an equal number of baths or showers, maids, bellmen, and telephones. The only other hotel available to "colored people" at the time was the Lincoln on Indiana Avenue. At the Liberty, three two-story houses behind the hotel served as short-term rentals for Club Harlem dancers and other entertainers; the nearby Green Parrot restaurant provided room-service meals. The main building still stands and houses senior citizens.

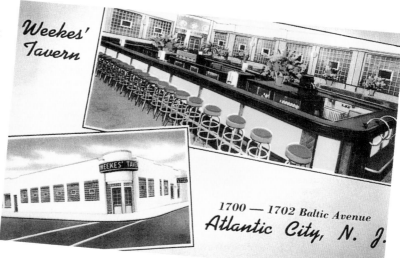

Weekes' Tavern

1700 — 1702 Baltic Avenue
Atlantic City, N. J.

LIBERTY HOTEL — 1519-21-23 Baltic Avenue — ATLANTIC CITY, NEW JERSEY

LIGHT BLUE

NAMED FOR A RUG SHOP,

Oriental Avenue boasted apartments, boarding houses, kosher delis and, during World War II, a Boardwalk coast-guard tower that kept an eye peeled for enemy subs.

Vermont and Connecticut Avenues ran perpendicular to Oriental a few blocks apart and also catered to a Jewish clientele. Absecon Lighthouse, now a tourist attraction but once a lifesaver for boats negotiating the tricky Absecon Inlet currents, dominated the early oceanfront between Vermont and Rhode Island Avenues.

The real estate was not expensive in this neighborhood at the far north of the island, but the properties were tidy and quite livable. On the MONOPOLY board, the Light Blues are in a sweet spot of low cost and decent return, giving investors more bang for the buck than their lower-cost neighbors on Dark Purple. The Light Blue trio is ranked second overall among the ten property groups, paying back 20.7 cents for a dollar invested each time an opponent completes a trip around the board. One favored strategy is to accumulate LBs early to raise cash for a more expensive purchase.

Absecon Lighthouse towered over a stretch of Victorian homes on Vermont Avenue just beyond a grassy area fronting the lighthouse. Before it retreated inland from both the ocean and Absecon Inlet (top), the lighthouse saved many a mariner from crashing or foundering his vessel. It was completed in 1857, three years after a northeaster sank the immigrant ship Powhattan and washed some 300 bodies ashore. Atlantic City founder Dr. Jonathan Pitney petitioned Congress for the funds, and Lieutenant George Gordon Meade—later of Civil War fame at Gettysburg—engineered the project, turning $35,000 into a 167-foot-tall structure whose beacon reached twenty miles to sea. Years later, it loomed over Vermont Avenue and the Pacific Avenue straightaway to the ocean.

CONNECTICUT AVENUE

VERMONT AVENUE

CHAN

ITING

PRICE $120

PRIC

ABSECON LIGHT HOUSE, ATLANTIC CITY, N. J.

Above, left, and opposite, top: Like the New Yorker and other hotels on Connecticut Avenue, Galen Hall advertised comfort and luxury, but went a step further in billing itself as a sanatorium for restoring health and vigor. To that end, it pumped ocean water into private rooms so that patrons could immerse themselves in salt baths. The Galen Hall "Exchange" (opposite, top) awaited revivified guests. Fittingly, the hotel was named for the influential Roman physician/philosopher Galen, whose mythology includes his being an attendant of the "healing god" Asclepius in the second century A.D.

EXCHANGE OF GALEN HALL, ATLANTIC CITY.

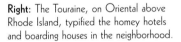

Right: The Touraine, on Oriental above Rhode Island, typified the homey hotels and boarding houses in the neighborhood.

The Touraine, Oriental above Rhode Island Ave., Atlantic City, N. J.
Misses Boyer & Thomas, Proprietors.

GRAND ATLANTIC HOTEL,
200 Rooms, 75 Private Baths,
Virginia Avenue near the Beach,
Atlantic City, N. J.

PENNSYLVANIA RAILROAD

VIRGINIA AVENUE

STATES AVENUE

PRICE $160

PRICE $140

PRICE $150

THIS TRIO OF PROPERTIES ranges

from the upper-crust States Avenue and St. Charles Place to the show business profile of Virginia Avenue. While St. Charles signified class and elegance, and States was graced by large Victorian summer homes and stabled horses, greasepaint Virginia met Mister Peanut at the Planters store on the Boardwalk and culminated in the Steel Pier, whose performers tended to bunk down the block when they weren't water-logged: the Diving Horse riders and aqua-acrobats landed at Hotel Virginia, and Tony Grant's "Stars of Tomorrow" twinkled at the Clarendon. Stage performers appearing at the nearby Apollo and Globe theatres also routinely sought accommodations in Virginia Avenue hotels and rooming houses.

The map has since been rewritten. States and St. Charles are gone, swallowed by the immensity of Showboat Casino Hotel. A small piece of States Avenue's once flowering medial strip remains, but not a trace of those fine old Victorians. Virginia's glitter has fled the footlights; a senior citizens high rise is the only prominent structure on the block. The Steel Pier, however, has been making a comeback, and these streets in the shadows of huge casino-hotels, are trying to do the same. In MONOPOLY land, the Light Purples are reasonably priced and profitable, ranked fourth for payoff percentage (17.7 cents on the dollar).

One of the many "modern" Virginia Avenue hotels of the day, the Grand Atlantic advertised creature comforts: private baths with hot running water, electric lights, and elevators.

ELECTRIC
COMPANY

ST. CHARLES
PLACE

PRICE $140

Sunday Evening

Grand March from "Athalia"......*Mendelssohn*
Overture—Zampa ....*Herold*
(a) The Lost Chord....................*Sullivan*
(b) Polish Dance ....*Scharwenka*
Grand Opera—Faust...................*Gounod*
'Cello Solo—Fond Recollections........*Popper*
                Mr. L. Bradac
Selection—Bohemian Girl...............*Balfe*
In Beauty's Bower (Idylle) ....*Bendix*
Humoresque ....*Dvorak*
Menuetto All'Antico ....*Karganoff*

Monday Evening

March—Military Spirit ....*Blon*
Valse—Wedding Dance ....*Lincke*
Fantasie—Les Noces de Figaro.........*Mozart*
(a) Somewhere a Voice Is Calling.......*Tate*
(b) Some Little Bird...................*Alstyne*
Norwegian Dance ....*Grieg*
Selection—Blue Paradise ....*Romberg*

Request Number

Maria, Mari.......................⎫
O, Sole Mio.......................⎬ *Capua*
Apache Love ....⎭ .....*Brockman*

Tuesday Evening

March—Mobilization ....*Wolianka*
Overture—Magic Flute...............*Mozart*
Valse—Marianna ....*Waldteufel*
(a) At Dawning.....................*Cadman*
(b) Peggy O'Neil....................*Dodge*
Grand Opera—La Boheme............*Puccini*

Request Number

Love's Joy (Liebesfreud).............*Kreisler*
Selection—Chu-Chin-Chow ....*Norton*
Yoo-Hoo ....*Jolson*

Wednesday Evening

Persian March ....*Strauss*
Valse—Caressante ....*Gabriel-Marie*
Overture—Barber of Seville...........*Rossini*
Fantasie—Lucia di Lammermoor.......*Donizetti*
(a) Serenade ....*Herbert*
(b) Sweetheart ....*Johnson*
Suite—Nell Gwyn Dances.............*German*
    (1) COUNTRY DANCE   (2) MERRYMAKERS

Request Number

Selection—The Kiss Waltz............*Ziehrer*
Learn to Smile, from "The O'Brien Girl"..*Hirsch*

MOSER'S GUEST HOUSE
2 DOORS FROM BOARDWALK
182 STATES AVENUE
ATLANTIC CITY, N. J.

LOBBY, DAVIS HOTEL, ST. CHARLES PL. AND BEACH, ATLANTIC CITY, N. J.   YETTA DAVIS, OWNERSHIP-MANAGEMENT

Above, left: Music was in the air at most of Atlantic City's major hotels, which featured bands in the afternoon and ballroom dancing at night. The St. Charles Hotel, situated between St. Charles Place and New Jersey Avenue at the Boardwalk, was a large beachfront hotel with, judging from the above program, aspirations of refinement. A 1952 fire showed no respect, however, destroying the hotel's wooden section and one of its "twin towers." Three other hotels were damaged in the fire, and the St. Charles was the only one to reopen.

Above, right: Beginning in the 1940s, many grand residences on States Avenue became guest houses, as the moneyed classes changed generations and domiciles, horses disappeared from the beach block, and the street-surface gravel was finally paved in 1948.

Left: Damask draperies, high-backed chairs, and grandfather clocks pressed the plush carpet in the lobby of the Davis Hotel on St. Charles Place. The raging '52 fire reduced this finery to ash.

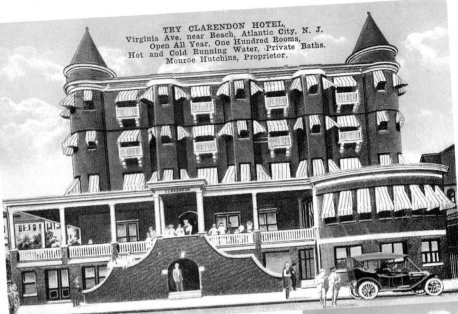

TRY CLARENDON HOTEL,
Virginia Ave. near Beach, Atlantic City, N. J.
Open All Year, One Hundred Rooms,
Hot and Cold Running Water, Private Baths.
Monroe Hutchins, Proprietor.

Left: The Hotel Clarendon was favored by the Steel Pier children's revue known as Tony Grant's "Stars of Tomorrow." Grant's showcase was a forerunner of TV youth performance competitions that featured the likes of beach-blanket movie star Frankie Avalon and Broadway "Annie" Andrea McArdle. The Clarendon stood across Virginia Avenue from the Grand Atlantic.

Right: Another gracious establishment on St. Charles was The Loraine, where, unfortunately, the destructive 1952 fire started. The conflagration spread to the adjacent St. Charles Hotel and other structures, ending an era on this quiet strip of seashore.

THE LORAINE,
ST. CHARLES PLACE
AND BEACH,
ATLANTIC CITY, N. J.

A. E. WAGNER, PROP.,
W. R. LAYTON, MGR.

THE ALBEMARLE HOTEL, VIRGINIA AVENUE NEAR BEACH, ATLANTIC CITY, N. J.

Left: The Albemarle Hotel, on the corner of Virginia and Pacific avenues, changed its name to the Wiltshire, the Absecon and, finally, the Canfield. It also changed its appearance several times and, at one point, had a first-floor drugstore and two exterior staircases leading from the porch to Pacific Avenue.

ORANGE

THE IRISH TRIED THEIR LUCK in midtown on St. James Place and on Tennessee and New York Avenues, which ran the entire width of the island. It was a neighborhood that balanced the rowdy with the religious. New York Avenue spotlighted Fort Pitt, a nightclub frequented by mobsters and molls and the G-men who chased them. Tennessee, on the other hand, offered St. Nicholas Church, whose expansion and architectural splendor mirrored the growth of the parish.

New York Avenue's bad-boy aspects were tempered by the Salvation Army building and the castle-like Morris Guards building, an armory named for Civil War veteran and Atlantic City surveyor Daniel Morris, who laid out the town's initial street grid and mapped the right-of-way for the Camden and Atlantic Railroad. Meanwhile, Tennessee Avenue's holiness was compromised by City Hall at Atlantic Avenue. Sandwiched by these two prime arteries, St. James Place, with its Irish Pub and Columbus Hotel, had the right flavor to draw people from Pennsylvania coal towns and other blue-collar burgs.

On the MONOPOLY board, these three properties get a lot of traffic, reflecting their location in the heart of the city. They are not too costly and the combination gives them the top payoff ranking of all the property groups (23.5 cents on the dollar). Some say that New York Avenue, the most expensive of the three, is the single most valuable property in the game.

NEW YORK AVENUE

TENNESSEE AVENUE

Now the Irish Pub, the Elwood Hotel also held court on St. James Place.

COMMUNITY
CHEST

ST. JAMES
PLACE

PE

Right: Architecturally, the Hotel Fredonia was no shrine, but ironically, the building stands while palatial wonders have vanished. In its heyday, it was where the Shriners stayed when they came to town.

Below: Atlantic City's second City Hall rose on the corner of Tennessee and Atlantic in 1901, succeeding the original building on the same site. The present City Hall is less than a block away.

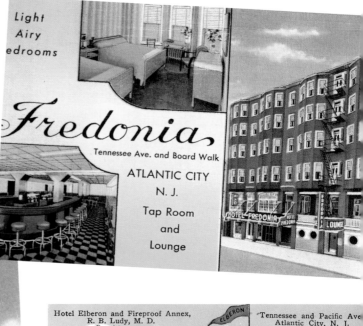

Light Airy Bedrooms

Fredonia

Tennessee Ave. and Board Walk

ATLANTIC CITY N. J.

Tap Room and Lounge

104 CITY HALL, ATLANTIC CITY, N. J.

Hotel Elberon and Fireproof Annex, R. B. Ludy, M. D. Proprietor.
"BEST MODERATE-PRICED HOTEL IN ATLANTIC CITY."

Tennessee and Pacific Ave Atlantic City, N. J.

Above: At Tennessee and Pacific, the Elberon was named after the New Jersey town where President James A. Garfield, only months after his election, was taken in 1881 for treatment following what would prove to be a mortal wound from an assassin's bullet. The hotel's life span lasted a lot longer than Garfield's brief presidency.

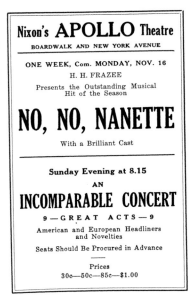
Left: The Apollo Theatre, at New York Avenue and the Boardwalk, was one of the nation's top tryout venues for Broadway-bound shows. In addition to the leading lights of the American stage, it hosted Al Jolson, Bill "Bojangles" Robinson, and vaudevillians such as W. C. Fields and the Marx Brothers. It was built by saltwater taffy king Joseph Fralinger, who named it after the God of Music and leased it to exhibitor Samuel Nixon. The costs of mounting *No, No, Nanette* forced producer Harry Frazee, who also owned the Boston Red Sox, to sell a baseball player named Babe Ruth to the New York Yankees.

Right: The Knights of Columbus built an elaborate clubhouse, complete with 110 rooms and a rathskeller, that became the Columbus Hotel at St. James and Pacific. The hotel emphasized its "modern fireproof construction" and "accommodations for ladies and gentlemen."

KNIGHTS OF COLUMBUS HOTEL, ATLANTIC CITY, N. J.

ST. JAMES AND PACIFIC AVES.   11627

LOUNGE AND LOBBY, HOTEL LEXINGTON

Hotel York at New York and Pacific Avenues

HOTEL YORK

Above and right: New York Avenue hotels included the York and the Lexington, the last with a restful lobby of wicker rockers and gauzy curtains. The seventy-room York was near Pacific Avenue. The Lexington was near the Boardwalk; a different Hotel Lexington was located at Arkansas and Pacific.

RED

VISITORS TO THE RED ZONE

were in for hot jazz and high living. On Kentucky Avenue, at the Wonder Garden bar and Grace's Little Belmont and, especially, Club Harlem, the music and the night never died. KY-at-the-curb was a pageant of limos dropping off high-stepping tuxes and furs. In the early days Club Harlem, at 32 North Kentucky, hid its gaming in the sideroom while showcasing the cream of America's black show business talent for a mostly white crowd.

The mighty Traymore Hotel dominated the Boardwalk at Illinois Avenue, and the exclusive Brighton Hotel on Indiana Avenue brewed a potent concoction known as Brighton Punch and served up space for swimming, dancing, and shuffleboard in its Boardwalk "casino"/solarium. The Monticello Hotel had a real casino (i.e.: gambling, albeit illegal), the Jefferson Hotel was reputedly owned by Al Capone, and during the Prohibition era, liquor stealthily traveled these roads from the back bays until it reached the rooftop beer gardens of such establishments as Craig Hall, where servers and imbibers could spot a raid coming and had enough time to make a getaway.

Elsewhere in the neighborhood, Negro League baseball legend John Henry "Pop" Lloyd trimmed the lawns at Indiana Avenue Elementary School years before he was finally recognized by the Hall of Fame. Just off the beaten path on Illinois Avenue sat the shop of rolling chair "inventor" William Hayday, bandleader Glenn Miller's pad at the Park Lane Apartments, and the residence of the Tisch family, owners of the Traymore in a time when hoteliers lived right near their livelihoods.

The three Reds, placed next to each other on the MONOPOLY board as they are in real Atlantic City, together with the Orange properties (New York, Tennessee, St. James) form the central area of both the city and the game board. The Red properties receive plenty of traffic, as they are adjacent to Free Parking, and a Chance "Advance" card sends extra visitors to Illinois. They are ranked third in payoff percentage (17.8 cents on the dollar), but that may not fully reflect their impact on the game. Experienced players will tell you that a Red portfolio often swings the tide as you get deeper into the game.

ILLINOIS AVENUE

INDIANA AVENUE

PRICE $240

PRICE $220

. N. J.

EXCHANGE OF HOTEL TRAYMORE, ATLANTIC CITY, N. J.

Not long after rendering the design for the Blenheim, architect William Price conceived the fourteen-story Hotel Traymore, a domed Moorish marvel that displaced a four-story boarding house of the same name. The first wing of the new brick hotel rose in 1906 and the entire structure at Illinois and the Boardwalk was completed in 1914, retaining the original cottage's name—that of the Irish birthplace and Maryland country estate of an early and honored guest. Also dubbed "Monarch by the Sea," the Traymore was a rehab center for convalescing servicemen during World War II. A good portion of its parking lot became an ice skating rink in wintertime.

CHANCE

KENTUCKY AVENUE

FR

PRICE $220

Club Harlem, the sun in the Kentucky Avenue constellation, was known for dazzling stage shows and supreme jazz musicianship. A roster of Who's Who among black entertainers played here for four decades: Billie Holiday, Cab Calloway, Billy Daniels, Sammy Davis Jr., "Moms" Mabley, and countless others. "Hot Lips" Page blew scorching trumpet notes and "Peg Leg" Bates danced better on one leg than anyone else on two. Meanwhile, chorus girls and sleek dancers, like those of the Sepia Revue and the Beige Beauts, raised blood pressures.

94—Hotel Brighton, Atlantic City, N. J.

On Indiana Avenue set back from the Boardwalk, the Brighton Hotel was built during the period when the city precluded construction of living quarters within 300 feet of the Great Wooden Way. Unlike many of its contemporaries, it did not expand its boarding facilities oceanward when regulations relaxed, though it did build the Brighton Casino, which offered a range of recreational activities and connected to the hotel via a long, narrow passageway. The Casino's world-famous punch packed a wallop of rye, rum, and brown sugar, and was so potent that women were allowed no more than two glasses per day. The Brighton was the first Atlantic City hotel to stay open year round, and was so exclusive that it screened guests before accepting them. Only guests of the Marlborough-Blenheim and Traymore Hotels could join Brighton guests for a glass of punch in the lounge, and then only if they showed a proper card of introduction. The Brighton's snootiness could be traced to its origins as a summer boarding house for upper-class Philadelphians. It was the seashore home of prominent financier and Philly blueblood Anthony J. Drexel Biddle.

The BRIGHTON
Atlantic City

Home of the World Famous Brighton Punch

CRAIG HALL, SOUTH ILLINOIS AVENUE, ATLANTIC CITY, N. J.

Writing Room, Craig Hall, South Illinois Avenue, Atlantic City, N. J.

Above: Craig Hall, at Illinois and Pacific, began life in 1897 as the Garden Hotel, a seven-story "skyscraper" launched by Philadelphia chemical magnate John Wyeth who had been frustrated by his inability to secure reservations at the Brighton. He sent a tally-ho to greet guests arriving by train. The hotel's name changed when the building was acquired by Robert D. Craighead, who offered French cuisine and a rooftop garden for elite gatherings but, being a strict prohibitionist, no liquor. Craighead was the first hotelier in Atlantic City to establish more affordable, "side street" rates. The hotel was demolished in 1933 and a post office erected on the site four years later is still there.

Left: Every hotel worth its weight in quill pens had a writing area that provided the atmosphere and paraphernalia for composing missives to send back home from the seashore. Here is Craig Hall's version.

YELLOW

THE YELLOW PROPERTIES move us to the suburbs. Atlantic Avenue, the longest on Absecon Island, runs the length of Atlantic City and then replaces Pacific Avenue as the last street paralleling the beach through the townships of Ventnor and Margate all the way to Longport. Trolley tracks wound through Atlantic; indeed, the breadth of the street was intended to provide sufficient space between trollies and skittish horses pulling carriages. Fashionable Tudor and Colonial homes, many of them still standing, lined Atlantic Avenue in the 'burbs. In Atlantic City proper, Atlantic Avenue, which was originally a cowpath, became known for fine dining and was the main commercial strip before the beach shifted toward the ocean, creating room for Pacific Avenue.

Ventnor Avenue joins Atlantic on a parallel trail toward Longport and also showcased stately summer homes but added more commercial properties.

Marvin Gardens, bane of fastidious historians and accurate spellers (see postcards), was christened "Marven Gardens" by city planners and mapmakers because of its location on the border between the cities Margate and Ventnor (Mar + Ven = Marven), but the game of MONOPOLY forever altered a vowel. When enthusiast Charles Todd copied the game board for Charles Darrow, Todd passed on the misspelled name "Marvin Gardens," which Darrow branded for eternity. Not even the U.S. Post Office has been able to rectify matters.

The Yellows command high rents and purchase prices in MONOPOLY, as you might expect in the suburbs. They have a payoff ranking of sixth, but insiders consider them to be pivotal properties in the late stages of a game.

Many times in her checkered career, Lucy the Elephant needed to keep a stiff upper tusk. The Atlantic Avenue timber-and-metal pachyderm, Margate's most visible landmark, was one of several such eye-poppers planned by developers in 1881 to attract land investors to the area referred to as "South Atlantic City." (Lucy's cousins showed up in Cape May and Coney Island.) She stood 65 feet from the top of her howdah and weighed 90 tons. Visitors would climb to the top and survey the real estate below. In later incarnations, Lucy was a tavern and a hotel before a long period of vacancy and deterioration yielded to relocation and preservation as a museum not far from her original watering grounds.

MARVIN GARDENS

PRICE $280

WATER WORKS

PRICE

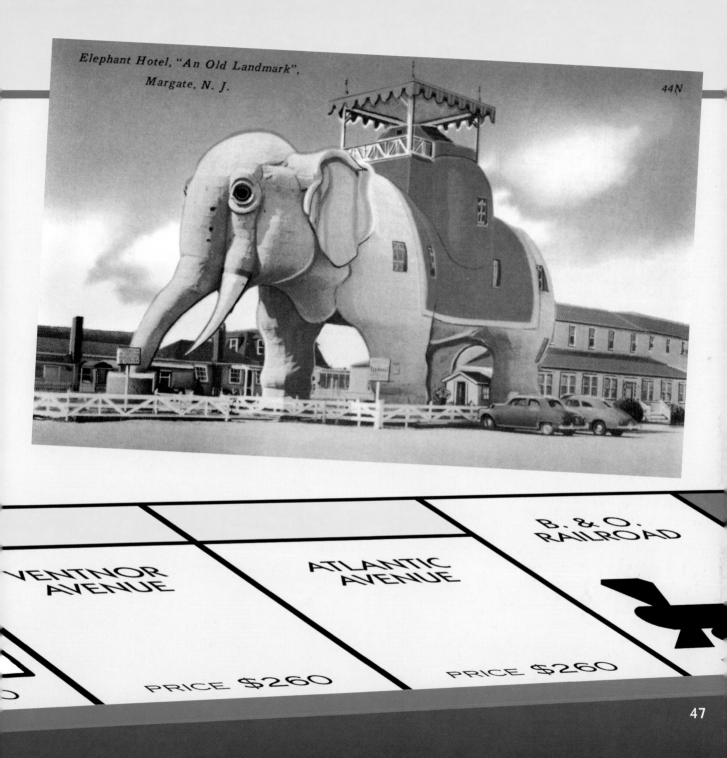

Elephant Hotel, "An Old Landmark",
Margate, N. J.

44N

VENTNOR AVENUE

PRICE $260

ATLANTIC AVENUE

PRICE $260

B. & O. RAILROAD

Advertisements fixed the Knife & Fork's location as "where the Atlantic meets the Pacific." The restaurant still sits at the confluence of Atlantic, Pacific, and Albany Avenues on the southern end of Atlantic City. Built in 1910 but leveled because of faulty nails and rebuilt two years later, the Knife & Fork Inn still offers sharp decor and riveting cuisine. When the Democrats held their national political convention in Atlantic City in 1964, the *New York Times* gave the Knife & Fork high marks, stimulating business at the restaurant and making it one of the few Atlantic City attractions to get favorable press during convention week.

Knife and Fork Inn, Atlantic City, N.
Atlantic and Albany Avenue
A. Cella, Prop.

218895

83

Hydrangeas in Full Bloom Along the Parkway, Atlantic City, N. J.

52957

The hydrangea, the official flower of Atlantic City, also abounds in Ventnor and Margate. It blooms in purple, pink, blue, and white, and gave rise to yet another strain of seashore beauty royalty: the Miss Hydrangea Queen.

MARVIN GARDENS, ATLANTIC CITY, N. J.—23

Above: Most postcards of Marvin Gardens use the MONOPOLY spelling "Marvin." This residential enclave of sparkling shrubs and serpentine streets mixed Tudor manses with Spanish villas and French chateaus, all adorned by well-tended shrubbery and billed as "homes of distinction." Hollywood played off that image by depicting a scruffier, pre-casino Atlantic City in the 1972 Jack Nicholson movie *The King of Marvin Gardens.*

MARGATE PARKWAY, ATLANTIC CITY, N. J.—32

Left: The ambitious thoroughfare that was to be Margate Parkway would have extended Ventnor Avenue through Atlantic City, but only a small portion of the project was completed. That seven-block stretch in the City of Margate, however, was a feast for the eyes and a smooth excursion for motorists. Large Tudor, Victorian, and Greco-Roman homes lined the sidewalk, and shrubs and statuary decorated the medial strip.

49

The **HOLMHURST** — ON BEAUTIFUL PENNSYLVANIA AVE. — ATLANTIC CITY, NEW JERSEY

6A-H757

SHOWING SECTION OF DINING ROOM — OPEN ALL YEAR

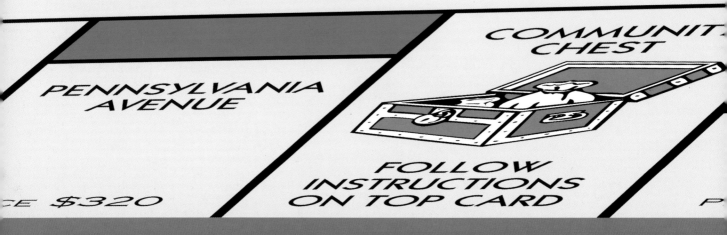

PENNSYLVANIA AVENUE

COMMUNITY CHEST

FOLLOW INSTRUCTIONS ON TOP CARD

CE $320

IT'S BACK UPTOWN for the Green properties of Pennsylvania and North Carolina Avenues, which frame Resorts Casino Hotel, the pioneer of Atlantic City's legal gambling era. Resorts has transformed the former Haddon Hall, completed in 1929, on the site of the original Haddon House, which was built in 1869. Elsewhere on North Carolina, the YWCA provided housing and support for young women, and churches reinforced the Quaker values of caring and decency.

Pacific Avenue, the third Green property, was laid in after the beach had expanded, allowing room for another street parallel to the coastline. Atlantic Avenue was already developed when Pacific became the first street from the beach. By the 1880s, large beautiful homes marked Pacific, but soon they were converted to, or replaced by, guest cottages. Pacific, North Carolina, and Pennsylvania were high-class streets in the 1920s and '30s, and stood up well to Atlantic City's decline four decades later. And, especially since they launched a new casino age, their color fits.

In MONOPOLY competition, the Greens—expensive and on the far side of the board—bide their time as the game progresses. Their average return on investment is on the low end (a payoff ranking of eighth), but the longer the game goes on, the greater their impact. Those high rents can knock out many a player.

The Holmhurst, second from the beach on Pennsylvania Avenue, was known for elegant service inside and out. Its dining room offered uniformed waitresses and white-linen service; outside at the front entrance, concrete blocks awaited the carriages of arriving guests.

NORTH CAROLINA AVENUE

PACIFIC AVENUE

$300

PRICE $300

The Colton Manor on Pennsylvania Avenue featured the 14th-floor Ship's Deck, a glass-enclosed salon and promenade deck that afforded a captain's-eye view of the ocean. During World War II, the hotel served as quarters for nurses working at nearby England General Hospital.

COLTON MANOR, PENNSYLVANIA AVENUE, ATLANTIC CITY, N. J.

Proprietor Mildred Fox dispatched a surrey to meet her lovestruck newlyweds at the railroad station and usher them to Pacific Avenue and her Fox Manor Hotel noted for its honeymoon suites. The hotel restaurant was aptly called the Surrey Room.

HOTEL LEXINGTON

PACIFIC AND ARKANSAS AVENUES
ATLANTIC CITY, N. J.

ENTRANCE FROM BEACH
CAPACITY 700
WHITE SERVICE

Above: A second Hotel Lexington in town (the other was on New York Avenue) had matching wings at Arkansas and Pacific Avenues—at one time reputed to be the only intersection in the country with a bar on each corner. The hotel was demolished in 1933.

Right: Many musical and vaudeville performers from the Steel Pier slumbered at the Seaside at the ocean end of Pennsylvania Avenue. The hotel housed Atlantic City's first radio station, WHAR, and the smooth sounds of the Seaside Trio, which provided daily afternoon concerts that were well attended. One regular listener liked to lead the band with her cigarette holder.

Radio Station WHAR

SEASIDE HOUSE

THE SEASIDE enjoys a far reaching reputation for the excellence and variety of its table, which receives the personal supervision of the management. Behind the entire personnel there is an understanding of the guest's requirements, catered to in a manner that adds a personal touch.

At the Ocean End of Pennsylvania Avenue

North Carolinia Ave. from Boardwalk showing
Chalfant Hotel & Haddon Hall,
Atlantic City, N. J.

The original Chalfonte Hotel, owned by Elisha Roberts, opened in 1868 and the "Haddon House" a year later. The modern, ten-story Chalfonte was built in 1904 as the city's first fireproof hotel. The massive structure known as Haddon Hall that rose in 1929 would be purchased five decades later by Resorts International and transformed into the city's first casino-hotel, which remains in operation. An enclosed bridge eventually connected the Chalfonte to Haddon Hall across North Carolina Avenue. The Chalfonte was noted for its March Musicales at which the likes of Metropolitan Opera star Lawrence Tibbett and cellist Pablo Casals performed. Haddon Hall hosted bandleader John Philip Sousa, and his stirring marches suited its history and personality. The building was converted to Thomas M. England General Hospital during World War II, housing more than two thousand patients at a time.

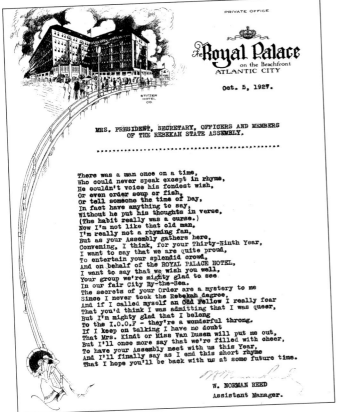

The Royal Palace
on the Beachfront
ATLANTIC CITY

STITZER
HOTEL
CO.

Oct. 5, 1927.

MRS. PRESIDENT, SECRETARY, OFFICERS AND MEMBERS
OF THE REBEKAH STATE ASSEMBLY.

. . . .

There was a man once on a time,
Who could never speak except in rhyme,
He couldn't voice his fondest wish,
Or even order soup or fish,
Or tell someone the time of Day,
In fact have anything to say,
Without he put his thoughts in verse,
(The habit really was a curse.)
Now I'm not like that old man,
I'm really not a rhyming fan,
But as your Assembly gathers here,
Convening, I think, for your Thirty-Ninth Year,
I want to say that we are quite proud,
To entertain your splendid crowd,
And on behalf of the ROYAL PALACE HOTEL,
I want to say that we wish you well,
Your group we're mighty glad to see
In our fair City By-the-Sea.
The secrets of your Order are a mystery to me
Since I never took the Rebekah degree,
And if I called myself an Odd Fellow I really fear
That you'd think I was admitting that I was queer,
But I'm mighty glad that I belong
To the I.O.O.F - they're a wonderful throng.
If I keep on talking I have no doubt
That Mrs. Kindt or Miss Van Dusen will put me out,
But I'll once more say that we're filled with cheer,
To have your Assembly meet with us this Year,
And I'll finally say as I end this short rhyme
That I hope you'll be back with us at some future time.

W. NORMAN REED
Assistant Manager.

Hotel La Fayette,
NORTH CAROLINA AVENUE,
ATLANTIC CITY, N. J.

Above: The Royal Palace was at the foot of Pacific Avenue at the Boardwalk. By rhyme or reason, as the above ode indicates, hotel management was always eager to please . . . especially when a large group was involved.
Right: Although it's not visible here, the Hotel La Fayette on North Carolina sported a downsized replica of the Eiffel Tower on top. The French flavor didn't stop a quartet of internationally famous Brits from checking in when they came to the shore as part of their American tour. Yes, the Beatles bunked here.

DARK BLUE

IN VINTAGE ATLANTIC CITY and in MONOPOLY land, this is the high-rent district. On the game board, if you land an opponent here after you've built a hotel on the property, you're likely to send him to the poorhouse.

An aristocratic-sounding name like Park Place tells you right away that you're among the rich. The Disston "cottage"—a summer estate of gables, gates, and gardens—once claimed these grounds, Henry Disston being the Philadelphia sawmill owner contracted to build the second Boardwalk. The beach frontage here between Indiana and Ohio Avenues has always been one of elegant greenery and dazzling light—rather than yet another building. Park Place equals open space.

As for the Boardwalk itself, the majestic hotels of yesteryear loomed like storybook structures, a testimony to architectural imagination. Some people suggest that the most elaborate of them—like the Traymore and the Blenheim (by the same architect's hand)—were inspired by, even modeled after, sandcastles that artisans built on the beach below. It's conceivable; sand art first appeared in the 1890s, and the spectacular hotels rose a decade later. Whatever the blueprint, most of the brick-and-mortar hotels ultimately met the same fate as the sandcastles on the beach.

BOARDWALK

PRICE $400

LUXURY TAX

PAY $75.00

PARK PLACE

PRICE $

3AH-1229

The Taj Mahal of the Atlantic City Boardwalk consisted of the palatial Blenheim, a melange of domes and monoliths, tethered to the gentle Marlborough with its deep porches and hooded windows. The Marlborough House (far right), which was built in 1902 and named after the home of England's Prince of Wales, had the look of the Swiss Alps transplanted to the seashore. Just three years after he commissioned William Price to design this rustic hotel, Quaker owner Josiah White had the Philadelphia architect draw up the specs for Atlantic City's first hotel to be constructed of reinforced concrete, a process improved by Thomas Edison when the Wizard wasn't lighting lights. Price responded with his ornate, opulent Blenheim, which was then tethered to the Marlborough by an elevated walkway. The Blenheim was the first Atlantic City hotel to equip every room with a private bath. Its celebrated afternoon teas inspired lyricist Irving Caesar to pen the words to the song "Tea for Two" in the hotel lobby in 1925.

PRICE $200   PRICE $320

51—Park Plaza and Central Hotels, Atlantic City, N. J.

The Plaza at Park Place was the jewel in Atlantic City's seashore crown. It fronted the skyscraping Claridge and was flanked by the exclusive Brighton (lower right) and Marlborough-Blenheim hotels. Its rich, startling greenery contrasted with the pastels of beach and Boardwalk, and its centerpiece was the Fountain of Light dedicated to the city by General Electric Company on the fiftieth anniversary of the Edison lightbulb.

The last and tallest of the Boardwalk's grand hotels, the twenty-floor Claridge was completed in 1930 and is one of the few to find new life in the casino age. Resembling a shorter, thickset cousin of the Empire State Building, it overlooks the plaza and fountain at Park Place, and at various times served as the Atlantic City headquarters of Frank Sinatra, Princess Grace of Monaco, legendary stage actress Katherine Cornell, Bishop Fulton J. Sheen, Bob "On the Road to Atlantic City" Hope, General Omar Bradley and, when he was vice president, Richard M. Nixon.

Claridge
PARK PLACE - INDIANA AVENUE
AND THE BEACH
Atlantic City

Right: Elisha Roberts, scion of a Philadelphia Quaker family that had boated across the Pond with William Penn, owned the Shelburne, the Atlantic City home of the town's top celebrity couple: stage diva Lillian Russell and rotund railroad magnate James Buchanan "Diamond Jim" Brady. Known for its graciousness and cuisine (Brady did like to eat), the Shelburne was also favored by Ethel Barrymore, Al Jolson, and composers Victor Herbert, Irving Berlin, and George M. Cohan. (The Yankee Doodle Dandy may have written his World War I anthem "Over There" right on the premises.) The original wooden hotel rose in 1869, but its development followed a familiar Atlantic City pattern, as more liberal building laws and new construction techniques allowed sturdier, larger, brick-and-concrete edifices to join existing structures. The mature Shelburne, with its steeple towering over a shorter front wing, seemed a building poised to take a bow.

149—THE SHELBURNE, ATLANTIC CITY, N. J.

3A-H1210

The Ambassador
ATLANTIC CITY

Left: The Ambassador was a hulking, block-long, sand-colored hotel smack up against the Ritz-Carlton. Built in 1919, it had seven hundred rooms; but President Woodrow Wilson's wartime edict restricted alcohol consumption (a forerunner of Prohibition), and there was no bar on the premises here until 1933. When in town, Paul Whiteman's jazzy orchestra, with a young vocalist named Bing Crosby, usually stayed here and enlivened the hotel's Grille Room with their music, as did other ensembles, one including a young Woody Herman. Town boss Nucky Johnson, whose headquarters was next door at the Ritz, also spent time at an Ambassador bungalow called the Santa Barbara.

114. HOTEL DENNIS, ATLANTIC CITY, N. J.

AS THERE is but one Atlantic City on all this great round globe, so there is but one Hotel Dennis in all this seaside city.

Hotels, like people, have a personality which distinguishes each from the other and cannot be successfully imitated—the predominating features of the Hotel Dennis being comfort, cheerfulness and an ample roominess that charms alike, the guest seeking rest, or the care-free globe trotter on pleasure bent—it caters to both, it satisfies both.

The Hotel Dennis started as a two-room house built by schoolmaster William Dennis before the Civil War. He sold the property to hoteliers who retained the name and kept expanding the site until it grew into the three-wing, mature structure that has survived and is now part of Bally's Park Place Casino. The blocky main building was attached to a pair of perpendicular adjuncts, giving the Dennis the look of a giant robot. In its heyday, the hotel adorned its famous St. Dennis Room with a timber-beamed ceiling, wall-sized murals, Oriental rugs, and a statue of the Saint himself.

THE PRESIDENT

ATLANTIC CITY, N. J.

The last Boardwalk hotel downbeach, the President was conceived as the "Summer White House" and named accordingly. Imposing oil canvasses of Lincoln and Washington dominated lobby walls. Built in 1926, the hotel featured a Presidential Suite on the top floor, but principal White House resident Silent Cal Coolidge basically said, "I do not choose to occupy," and that was that. During World War II training exercises, gunners crouched with machine guns perched on the hotel roof just above the president-less suite. In peacetime, the President attracted island-wide interest with championship swimming meets at its indoor pool.

Prominent seashore architect Vivian Smith, (his flair was evident in the Elks Club building on Virginia), designed the regal Breakers, whose rooftop garden and magisterial entrance faced Garden Pier at New Jersey Avenue and the Boardwalk. By the late 1920s, the hotel combined Smith's new front building with the dining room and lobby of the existing, wooden Hotel Rudolf, a five-story frame structure. An interesting scenario in Breakers history: One author claims that some mobsters in town for the May 1929 "crime lords convention" were turned away by the hotel because they were Jewish! Al Capone, who was not, reportedly threw a fit. Years later, and for much of its lifetime, the Breakers was a kosher hotel.

THE BREAKERS, ATLANTIC CITY, N. J.

Electric Company

Thomas Edison's incandescent light bulb was seven years old, and his generating station on Pearl Street in New York was three years younger, when The Electric Light Company of Atlantic City was incorporated in 1886. The company proceeded to build a powerhouse in Tucker's Alley just off the intersection of Baltic and Kentucky Avenues, bring incandescence to an array of new light standards on the Boardwalk, and gobble up every South Jersey electrical utility in sight as Atlantic City and the region grew in tandem. The netherworld of gas-flamed lamps was history; the age of the kilowatt was here for keeps.

The Boardwalk lit up like a firecracker that never stopped burning. Edison himself designed the pastel lighting that suffused Captain John Young's

FOUNTAIN OF LIGHT, ATLANTIC CITY, N. J.—40

mini-palace on Million Dollar Pier. Electricity brought signs-as-spectacle to the Boardwalk, as the 215-foot-long Chesterfield sign alternated color explosions atop Steeplechase Pier, an electric diver in a Jantzen swimsuit knifed into the ocean, and Million Dollar Pier ran electrified horse races round the huge oval that was the Seagram's sign. And it wasn't just lights that drew on this new source of power. Ranges, refrigerators, irons, vacuum cleaners . . . electricity was synonymous with civilization.

The electrical charge in Atlantic City is more potent than ever, as today's casino-hotels are a riot of light inside and out. Great animated signs at the city's gateway hail arriving visitors, and inside the spacious

Left: Park Place's luminous Fountain of Light, dedicated by the local electric company, celebrated the Golden Jubilee of Edison's invention.
Above: Atlantic City Electric Company.

gaming arenas, oceans of slot machines mesmerize with their continuously blinking lights.

Electric Company and Water Works, the utility properties in MONOPOLY, don't dazzle with a big payoff but do provide a decent return on a low investment, meeting the expectations of an investor in utility stocks. When both utilities are owned, rental income increases by two-and-a-half times. That's a nice dividend.

ATLANTIC CITY MOON.

Water Works

At first there were just shallow wells and rain cisterns. Then water from the mainland became a valued commodity for sale. Finally, the Atlantic City Water Works Company organized in 1882 to pipe artesian well water from the mainland into the island, giving the resort its first supply of running water. Six years later, a new company tapped local wells for the same purpose. The two companies were consolidated into a municipal water department in 1895.

A century later, as a burgeoning gaming industry made ever increasing demands on utilities, the seashore water supply was growing more fragile. Saltwater encroachment was one culprit, and desalination, though expensive, was being considered as an option in some areas. Atlantic City's water supply is still fed mostly by mainland aquifers, and environmental pressures at the seashore will continue to test local and state leadership.

Above: Park Place, the Boardwalk, the Marlborough-Blenheim Hotel, and a fingernail moon are lit by night.
Left: Hot and cold running water was one of the first amenities trumpeted by Atlantic City hotels, some of which pumped ocean water into the tub to give patrons a healthful splash of surf with no sand.

THE DECKS OF CARDS that repre-

sent Chance and Community Chest add extra spice and risk to the game of MONOPOLY. Just when your bank account is fattening and you think you're on your way to riches and power, you land on a Chance or Community Chest space (there are three of each), draw from the corresponding deck, and get hit with a big bill or are sent to an opponent's property where you have to pay through the nose. Or maybe your fortunes have been plummeting and you find yourself the beneficiary of a generous bequest. Of course, the same boost or reversal can happen to other players.

Early Atlantic City did have a "community chest"

that was a forerunner of such social service organizations as the United Way. When you land on MONOPOLY's Community Chest, you can be sure that money will change hands—but you may not be on the receiving end. As for Chance, Atlantic City has always been a gambler's paradise, and the same possibility applies when you find yourself on the space with the big question mark.

One Chance card, for example, moves you instantly to the Boardwalk property, which might be a site you want to buy to complete your financial empire. Or it may already belong to your opponent and have a hotel sitting on it, in which case you may be staring bankruptcy in the face.

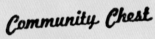

MARLBOROUGH-BLENHEIM HOTEL AND BOARDWALK AT NIGHT. ATLANTIC CITY. N. J.

75

60947

Marlborough-Blenheim Hotel and Boardwalk at Night—A nighttime
stroll on the Boardwalk complete with rolling chairs and grand hotels.

Take a Walk on the Boardwalk

Taking a walk on the Boardwalk in Atlantic City was an excursion into a wonderland of grand hotels, amusement piers stocked with colorful rides and marquee performers, and arcades full of games and sweet treats of every description. The Boardwalk was part avenue, part grandstand.

It began when hotel keepers and railroaders growing weary of sand tracked onto rugs and seats asked for an esplanade, portable or otherwise, to keep busy feet off the sand. The first one, a mile long but only 10 feet wide, was erected in 1870. It was built in sections, and the whole affair was dismantled and stored at the end of the season. The city council called it a "board walk." It would become the distinguishing feature of Atlantic City and many subsequent seashore resorts.

During the next quarter-century, Atlantic City replaced its Boardwalk four times due to storm damage and commercial growth. The "permanent" 1896 walk, 60 feet wide for most of its length and girded with steel, stretched more than four miles down the coast. There have been numerous repairs since, but this structure is essentially the Boardwalk of today, and with a capital "B," as the city gave it street status.

With the sturdy Boardwalk rimming the beach, the siren call "Sand in your Shoes" became more metaphorical than literal. Of course, heartier shoregoers did want the sand between their toes and the waves slapping their shoulders. For them, a phalanx of bath houses on the Boardwalk offered freshwater to clean the skin and towels to dry it. Sunbathers were well advised not to fry their epidermises—guidelines posted by the lifesaving Beach Patrol called for specified, gradual exposure for "safe" suntanning.

Two cultures sat side by side here at the edge of the continent. The Boardwalk, processional and dressy, belonged to the world of grand hotels which rose from a graceful nineteenth-century sensibility and then added bulk, glamour, and architectural awe in the twentieth. On the Boardwalk's ocean side, where great elongated piers glittered over the Atlantic, the cry of the barker and the lure of spectacle held sway.

The Boardwalk hotels formed the classic Atlantic City skyline of yesteryear, the one that graced a million salt water taffy boxes. Meanwhile, the beachtop boulevard was a rendezvous for sweethearts almost from the start, with rolling

A Plank Shad and a Chicken.

chairs increasing the chances for romance. Sometimes movement on the Boardwalk turned formal, as with the Miss America Pageant and the annual Easter Parade. Sometimes it was athletic, as in the fancy skating of the Ice Capades, or a sea of soldiers doing calisthenics—each of these activities inside Convention Hall. During World War II, beach and Boardwalk became training grounds.

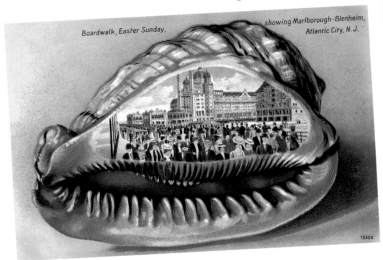

Boardwalk, Easter Sunday, showing Marlborough-Blenheim, Atlantic City, N.J.

Above: Larger-than-life comic figures on the Boardwalk have always greeted visitors. The familiar Mister Peanut, a natty soul with hat and cane, promoted Planters' snacks and was regarded as one of the family by vacationers. Here, a landed upright fish and a young lady make an interesting liaison.
Left: Framed by a seashell and backed by the Marlborough-Blenheim, a dense crowd in its Sunday finery promenades along the Boardwalk during the seashore's annual Easter Parade. The tradition began in 1876, the country's centennial, and soon became a showcase for the latest fashions, a barrage of bonnets and feathers and lace. The Boardwalk Easter Parade was one of several promotions—the Miss America Pageant being another—conceived by civic leaders to boost business in Atlantic City during the "shoulder" seasons before and after summer. Seven decades after the inaugural parade, African-American residents organized their own dress-up off the Boardwalk on Arctic Avenue.

But less sobering times would return. Amusement rides had been a staple of the Boardwalk and they started spinning again over the ocean. Built in the late nineteenth and early Twentieth centuries, the great amusement piers had enough eye-candy to sate even those with short attention spans. Loaded to the gills with fun ways to spend your money, the Heinz, Garden, Steel, Steeplechase, Central, and Million Dollar Piers were a feast for the young and young-at-heart.

Elsewhere on the Boardwalk, more legit entertainment made Atlantic City Broadway's top tryout town. The Apollo, Globe, and B. F. Keith theaters were the prime venues, and virtually every leading light of the American stage strode those boards in the 1910s and '20s. Art had its place on the beach side as well, as sand sculptors turned mounds of sand into depictions of patriotic and religious themes.

Beach and Boardwalk formed a seaside circus. While diving horses performed on the Steel Pier, riding horses cantered in the wet sand, kicking up surf rather than turf. And never was there a shortage of stunts calculated to catch the public eye or satisfy some strange individual yearning: the flagpole sitters, the buried alive routine, kangaroo fighters, the giant Underwood typewriter at the Garden Pier, the national Skee Ball tournament, men shot out of cannons, men dropped out of blimps, and in 1973, as proponents of casino gambling were already mustering their forces, a world MONOPOLY tournament, complete with a giant game board.

In this early scene of a teeming Boardwalk, ocean breakers rush to shore and the Brighton Hotel's "casino" beckons (upper right). The Brighton Casino was not a gaming house, but a solarium for reading, resting, recreating, and socializing.

549:—Plenty of Push in Atlantic City, N. J.

Above: Some chose to ride, rather than walk, the Boardwalk. Rolling chairs, which evolved from the wheelchairs that helped invalids and recuperating patients to a dose of salt air, were first rented at the hardware store of one William Hayday, but the heyday of the rolling chair was ushered in by Philadelphia manufacturer Harry Shill in the 1880s when he introduced canopied conveyances with signature swan-like fronts. Hundreds of city-licensed chair stands populated the Boardwalk, a song celebrated "a maiden in a little rolling chair . . . salty breezes through her curly locks of hair," and eventually, electric chairs droned next to those still driven by human muscle. Whatever the power source, the rolling chair was a seat for celebrity or commoner, and a smooth effortless excursion by the ocean's doorstep.

Right: An afternoon stroll on the boards and the beach.

YOUNG'S NEW MILLION DOLLAR PIER, ATLANTIC CITY, N. J.

68

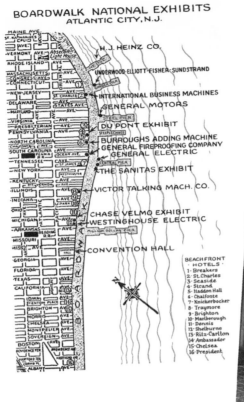

BOARDWALK NATIONAL EXHIBITS
ATLANTIC CITY, N.J.

H. J. HEINZ CO.

UNDERWOOD-ELLIOTT-FISHER-SUNDSTRAND

INTERNATIONAL BUSINESS MACHINES
GENERAL MOTORS
DU PONT EXHIBIT
BURROUGHS ADDING MACHINE
GENERAL FIREPROOFING COMPANY
GENERAL ELECTRIC
THE SANITAS EXHIBIT
VICTOR TALKING MACH. CO.

CHASE VELMO EXHIBIT
WESTINGHOUSE ELECTRIC

CONVENTION HALL

· BEACH FRONT ·
- HOTELS -
1- Breakers
2- St. Charles
3- Seaside
4- Strand
5- Haddon Hall
6- Chalfonte
7- Knickerbocker
8- Traymore
9- Brighton
10- Marlborough
11- Dennis
12- Shelburne
13- Ritz-Carlton
14- Ambassador
15- Chelsea
16- President

Major American corporations used the Boardwalk as a platform to showcase their latest wares and technological advancements. In pier pavilions or hotel exhibit rooms, the likes of General Motors, General Electric, and DuPont caught the public's eye with their new products and demonstrations, and the Boardwalk became a kind of permanent state fair.

Giant Gate Valve Forming Main Entrance to Crane National Exhibit.

USE CRANE VALVES

Boardwalk, Atlantic City, N. J.

42—Sculptures, Made Out of Sand Only, Along the Beach, Atlantic City, N. J.
COPYRIGHT, 1911, BY HERMAN BECHER, N. Y

Professional sand sculpting originated in Atlantic City in 1897, as beach artists began encouraging Boardwalk sightseers to make "donations" as a token of their appreciation. Historic, religious, and naturalistic subjects were depicted by the sculptors, who sometimes added a dash of cement to the mix to combat erosion by sea and air. Such reinforcement did not deter the 1944 hurricane, however, and it wiped out the sandy gallery forever.

24. NET HAUL, YOUNG'S MILLION DOLLAR PIER, ATLANTIC CITY, N. J.

3 CAPT. YOUNG'S RESIDENCE ON MILLION DOLLAR PIER,

ATLANTIC CITY, N. J.

Above: Commerce was its own attraction, as the twice-daily landing of deep-sea fish at Million Dollar Pier held a fascination for onlookers. The Net Haul became as popular as amusement rides and stage acts.

Right: Captain John Lake Young's residence was the jewel box on the chiffonier that was Million Dollar Pier. Located midway down the pier, it was a palace-in-miniature, one that commanded a singular address: Number One, Atlantic Ocean. Thomas Alva Edison, a friend and fishing partner of the flamboyant seashore impresario, designed soothing pastel lighting for both the inside and outside of the three-story Venetian villa which featured a frontyard full of marble statuary and, in general, the stuff of which dreams are made.

Right: The Garden Pier celebrated performance with zany comedians, feats of daring, and stirring music. That's the B. F. Keith Theatre straight ahead, beyond the pier's centered floral displays and flanking pavilions. The Keith dangled Harry Houdini from the heights, provided floor space for a tango teacher named Rudolph Valentino, and hosted the maiden outing of a beauty contest that grew into the Miss America Pageant. A later incarnation of the Garden Pier featured an outdoor, art deco band shell that still stands though it is not active. Today, much of the site has been recast as the city Historical Museum and Art Center.

Below: The long view of the City's uptown piers and a packed Boardwalk.

237 The Garden Pier, Atlantic City, N. J.

Steel Pier, Garden Pier and Heinz's Pier, Atlantic City, N. J.

Copyright by Atlantic Foto Service.

GIANT UNDERWOOD TYPEWRITER, UNDERWOOD GARDEN PIER EXHIBIT, ATLANTIC CITY, N. J.   103215

THE CLUCKING CLERK
Postcards 10¢

THE CLUCKING
CLERK

Above: Long before computers, there was a dinosaur called the typewriter, and this fourteen-ton Underwood was truly dinosaur-sized. Operated via remote control, it clacked away in the Garden Pier's "Products and Progress" pavilion from 1916 to 1934 before moving to Convention Hall and, eventually, the scrap heap. When intact, it was 21 feet wide and 18 feet high—no laptop, to be sure.

Right: Will Work for Birdseed: Some Boardwalk establishments kept payrolls low by having "performing animals" handle some of the concession duties. This "Clucking Clerk," dispensing dime postcards on the Steel Pier, was trained for its Atlantic City gig by an animal psychologist in Hot Springs, Arkansas.

Don't Miss a Visit to George C. Tilyou's

STEEPLECHASE
"The Funniest Place on Eearth"

35 NEW AND NOVEL

ATTRACTIONS

DANCING

Every Afternoon at 3.15
Every Evening at 8.30

The piermeister whose promotional flair rivaled John Young's was George Cornelius Tilyou, who virtually invented New York's Coney Island and whose Steeplechase Pier in Atlantic City compiled a wild assortment of amusements. Transformed from refined Auditorium Pier into Steeplechase—The Funny Place, The Mirth Place of the Nation, it was filled with dizzying rides and a madcap mentality. But Steeplechase had its own difficulties staying upright. Fire consumed it and its 215-foot-long Chesterfield sign, the largest electric sign in the world, in 1932. The Tilyous rebuilt to great success, but fire would strike again five decades later. Plans for yet another pier have not advanced beyond the drawing board.

The H. J. Heinz Company, with its meal-ticket fifty-seven fabulous flavors, wanted to be certain that homemakers had ample modern facilities in which to spread the goodies. Hence, the Heinz Ocean Pier Kitchens exhibit that tracked the evolution of culinary travail across the globe. Here, the wonders of the "modern" kitchen are open for inspection: built-in cupboards, linoleum floors, indirect lighting, and electric refrigerator, range, and dishwasher. Nine separate model kitchens reflected different historical periods in different countries, including early Dutch, English, Spanish, French, Colonial American, and Arcadian.

A shingled, six-room Model Home was part of a larger display on the Central Pier, which stood on the same real estate that had supported Captain John Young's Ocean Pier, which, in turn, had supplanted Applegate's, the city's first amusements pier of consequence. Central Pier eschewed amusements for commercial exhibits, and this exemplar of the Federal Housing Administration fit the specs.

EXHIBIT OF GENERAL MOTORS

MINEVITCH & HIS RASCALS
3 PHOTOPLAYS
MINSTRELS

STEEL PIER

STEEL PIER

WM O'NEAL IN PERSON
ALL FOR ONE ADMISSION

DE LUXE VAUDEVILLE—MODERN MINSTRELS
FEATURE PHOTOPLAYS—BABY ANIMAL ZOO
CONGRESS OF DAREDEVIL CIRCUS ACTS
LUXURIOUS THEATRES CONTINUOUS SHOWS

FOX
PICTURES

PHIL EMERTON HENRIETTA CROSMAN
& HIS DIAMONDS GEORGE RAFT CLIVE BROOK IN "PILGRIMAGE"

DIVING HORSES

ENTRANCE

TIGERS

A VACATION IN ITSELF

Left: Of all the Atlantic City vintage piers, the Steel Pier is the one name that remains fixed in the national consciousness. Host to big bands (including those headed by Benny Goodman, Harry James, Gene Krupa, Glenn Miller, Tommy Dorsey, Duke Ellington, and Count Basie), big singers from Sinatra on down, the famed Marine Ballroom, Ed Hurst's "Steel Pier Radio Show," early Miss America Pageants, Depression-era dance marathons, diving bells, and diving horses, it was dubbed the "Show Place of the Nation" and part of it became a showroom for General Motors' newest line of cars. Built of wood in 1898, the Steel Pier now sits on concrete pilings and is enjoying a renaissance. **Below:** General Motors trotted out its latest models for public display on the Steel Pier, but this vintage Pontiac is superimposed on a scene that looks south toward the Million Dollar Pier, with the Marlborough-Blenheim and Shelburne hotels on the right.

THE PONTIAC BIG SIX LANDAULET SEDAN

Greetings From
The Steel Pier

NIGHT VIEW OF THE FAMOUS STEEL PIER

Atlantic City,
New Jersey—35

2 Men Shot from
a Giant Cannon

CROWDS INTENTLY WATCHING SENSATIONAL CIRCUS PERFORMERS

High Diving Horses
with Girl Riders

At the ocean end of Steel Pier, fearless steeds and riders leaped from a 40-foot tower into a deep pool of water, unleashing a monster splash and crowd gasps louder than the ocean's roar. The High-Diving Horses act had been invented by frontiersman Dr. William Frank Carver, friend and associate of Buffalo Bill and known as the world's greatest rifle shot. Deadeye Doc brought his divers from the county fair circuit to the Steel Pier for a fifty-year run beginning in 1928. His marquee diver and daughter-in-law, Sonora Webster Carver, launched the show in Atlantic City and continued to perform long after being blinded by a diving accident. In addition to the diving duos, Steel Pier showcased an entire "water circus" of daffy divers, bathing beauties, and Rex the Wonder Dog riding an aquaplane.

5461-29

March king John Philip Sousa played the Steel, Million Dollar, Steeplechase, and Garden Piers, as well as Haddon Hall, and always drew throngs to the Boardwalk to see and hear his band. He began in 1903 at Steeplechase, where owner George Tilyou booked him for free. Soon enough, the Sousa band became a hot ticket and its infectious march tunes part of the musical fabric of America. Through the 1920s, Sousa, with his captain's hat and erect bearing at the podium, was an Atlantic City fixture.

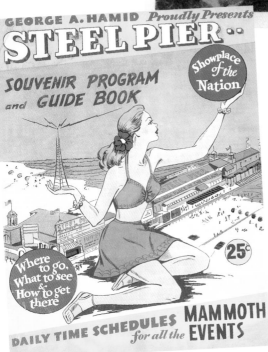

Steel Pier stages hosted marquee names like Frank Sinatra and Ella Fitzgerald, and lesser known performers who brought color and variety, such as Tony Grant's Stars of Tomorrow, Dicky Do and the Don'ts, the Diving Collegians, the Binswanger Bathing Beauties and, above, the Hawaiians.

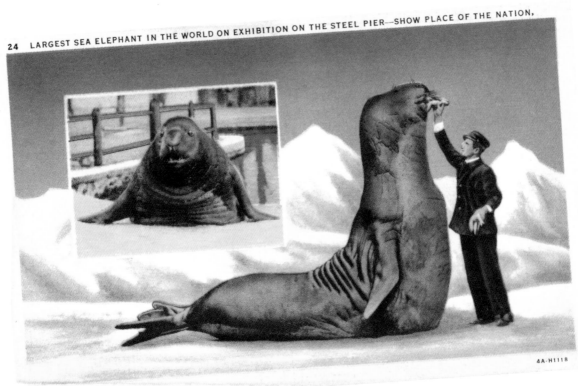

ATLANTIC CITY, N. J.

4A-H111B

Marine creatures were attractions at Steel Pier. Fortunately, these sizable sea elephants feasted on fish rather than their handlers.

18290

A BEACH BILLY-HO

ATLANTIC CITY, N.J.

THE SPEARMAN PUB. CO.   ATLANTIC CITY, N.J.

This is the way children drive along

Beach life was a bit more rustic and wide-open in the early days, as these scenes show. Young ladies could hitch a ride on a goat-drawn cart, while horses congregated near the hulking Traymore Hotel. Well-to-do residents, notably those living on States Avenue, stabled their horses right at home—the beach was just a horseshoe toss away. Primetime for riding was the winter season, when the beach was desolate and the level sand at the shoreline was hard and smooth. Despite the city's prohibition, horses were seen on the Atlantic City beach as late as the 1940s before four-legged sandcombers (aside from the occasional dog) headed inland for good.

Romance was a calling card of Atlantic City from the very beginning. In a Victorian age, the resort suspended the stiff rules of socialization and loosened inhibitions. The very first amusements pier, Applegate's, boasted a "Lover's Pavilion," and several spots along the Boardwalk gained reputations as rendezvous points. At least for the summer, the sand and planks were great levelers, mingling the social classes, sometimes with a hint of scandal.

Greetings from Atlantic City

What the waves saw

GREETING FROM
HEINZ
PIER
ATLANTIC CITY, N.J.

A Rescue at Atlantic City, N. J.

Copyright 1907 Illustrated Postal Card & Nov. Co. N.Y.

"The Lock Step on the Beach" Atlantic City, N. J.

Above: The Atlantic City Beach Patrol, organized in 1892, grew out of limited lifeguard services established twenty years earlier. Beach-based medical services appeared in the early 1900s, and a hospital tent soon rose on the sand. Familiar rescue boats and lookout stands have long signaled assurance to beachgoers. On a lighter note, cantankerous comic W. C. Fields and, later, the comedy team of Dean Martin and Jerry Lewis took advantage of the patrol's high profile by staging mock "drownings" to attract attention and publicize their local appearances.

LARGEST CONVENTION HALL IN THE WORLD. SEATING CAPACITY 40,000, BALL ROOM 5,000   475-29

M.M.%M.C.B.
CONVENTION
ATLANTIC CITY 1907

Above: Completed in 1929, Atlantic City Auditorium—commonly known for many years as Convention Hall and now called Boardwalk Hall—was the world's largest building without roof posts and pillars, and still houses the planet's largest pipe organ. During the World War II years, it answered a bugle call and served as a base of operations for the U.S. Army. Still active, the hall has hosted thousands of memorable events, including the Miss America Pageant, the Ice Capades, national collegiate football rivalries, heavyweight boxing championships, and in 1964, the Democratic National Convention that nominated sitting President Lyndon Baines Johnson. Indeed, the mammoth building was built for conventions, which were correctly seen as a prime vehicle for stoking the local economy. And that is what happened, as surgeons and Shriners, farmers and factory workers, came to the city and brought their families . . . and their wallets.

Left: Novelty studios along the Boardwalk featured painted sets through which a visitor could insert his or her head for a comic, sometimes dramatic picture. This set appears to have been destined for a railroad convention.

Greetings from Atlantic City
IT'S THE SUNSHINE TOWN
WHERE EVERYBODY
LAUGHS

THE FAULTS OF OUR
BROTHERS WE WRITE
ON THE SAND
THEIR VIRTUES UPON THE
TABLET OF LOVE AND
MEMORY

HELLO BILL!

THE SAND ARTIST AT WORK ON THE BEACH, ATLANTIC CITY, N. J.

The Elk Model in sand is an original idea of Frank B. Hubin. The modeling being done by James J. Taylor the originator of pictures in the sand. The photograph was taken by Adam Freund. This model of an Elk is acknowleged to be the finest sand picture ever made.

Above: The Brotherhood of Elks was one of the many groups that held their conventions in Atlantic City. The message in sand to Brother Bill reads, "The fault's of our brothers we write on the sand. Their virtues upon the tablet of love and memory." **Right:** One body fits all (heads).

83

The snack of choice along the Boardwalk was salt water taffy, and entrepreneur Joseph Fralinger turned the sticky confection into a seashore icon. The tale of how it originated, perhaps apocryphal, is that when a storm surge soaked a taffy stand, proprietor David Bradley renamed his stock accordingly. The name, though, received no copyright, and it was Philadelphia transplant Fralinger who marketed the non-nutritious mix of sugar, cream, and water (not sea water, either) to mass popularity, even providing detailed instructions to get it securely from wrapper to taste buds.

Community Chest

YOU HAVE WON SECOND PRIZE IN A BEAUTY CONTEST COLLECT $10

© 1936 PARKER BROTHERS, INC.

There she Is . . . and by today's standards, rather modest-looking. A Miss America contestant towers over a beach crowd of yesteryear, with the Keith Vaudeville Theater on the Garden Pier (site of the first "pageant") in the background.

Second Prize in a Beauty Contest

Atlantic City was a natural setting for beauty contests, and the eventual financial payoff for many contestants went well beyond the ten dollars doled out to runnersup by MONOPOLY's Community Chest. With the ocean as a backdrop, increasingly bare limbs flashing in the sun, and the broad Boardwalk tailor-made for a parade, the atmosphere was ripe.

The impulse bore fruit with beauty contests of every stripe: Miss Hydrangea Queen, Miss Beach Patrol, Miss Submarine, Miss Prettiest Waitress, Miss Steel Pier, Miss Atlantic City, Little Miss Atlantic City. There was even a Miss International Nude and, at the other end of the scale, a Ms. Senior Citizen. The most enduring of them all, of course, was Miss America, which, having survived a feminist attack in the late 1960s, still stages its annual tug-of-war between sex appeal and wholesomeness.

It began as the Inter-City Beauty Contest in 1921 and grew to be a national spectacle. The maiden outing tested just eight amateur contestants, but that number increased by fifty the following year. Eventually, pageant organizers settled on one entry per state rather than a

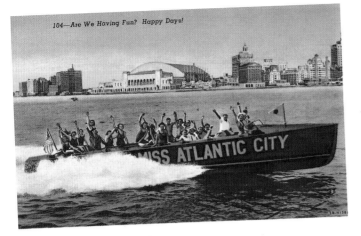

Above: Miss Atlantic City speedboats were part of Captain Starn's armada of sightseeing vessels that went from inlet to ocean and as far south as the President Hotel. A photographer was always on hand to snap and sell prints to eager mates, who were often joined by a visiting celebrity for the ride. The Starn's operation ferried an estimated one million sightseers up and down the oceanfront each season. **Right:** Queen of the beauty queens, Marilyn Monroe was a rising young star in Hollywood at the time she grand-marshaled the Miss America Pageant parade on the Boardwalk in 1952. **Opposite, bottom:** The confection clings to her swimsuit, as a Salt Water Taffy Queen exults by the ocean. Of all of Atlantic City's beauty pageant winners, she was the one with the most stick-to-it-ive-ness.

jumble of local beauties, as Atlantic City officials encouraged them to create an event of national stature in order to extend the summer season in a big way.

That is exactly what happened as the post-Labor Day pageant moved from the Garden Pier to Million Dollar Pier to Steel Pier and, finally, Convention Hall, attracting celebrities, sponsors, and television contracts along the way. In 1945, New York contestant Bess Myerson played a concert piano, looked great doing it, and won the crown as a prelude to becoming a top television personality. In 1952, parade grand marshal Marilyn Monroe sat high on the backseat of a roofless auto and stretched her arms toward the heavens. Three years later, rookie master of ceremonies

Bert Parks gave the winner a sendoff by singing a new song, "There She Is, Miss America," which became the event's eternal theme song. Hollywood fixed its eyes on the pageant, offering screen tests and careers to the chosen. Contestants Joan Blondell and Vera Miles didn't capture the crown but did win studio contracts.

Anointed queens of other Atlantic City beauty pageants also beat a path to moviedom. Ali MacGraw was Haddon Hall's entrant in the 1957 Prettiest Waitress Contest long before her star turn in Love Story. As another song, "On the Boardwalk in Atlantic City" (debuted in the 1946 Miss America Pageant), suggested, the seashore was the place to catch your eye.

House Repairs

For many years, Atlantic City kept its prime real estate values high and discouraged small-scale development by selling Boardwalk land in 10x30-foot lots but permitting construction only on minimum 30x30 parcels.

This often compelled developers to acquire more land if they, in fact, wanted to build on the property, or if they sought to block development by a competitor. In the latter case, subsequent "horse trading" would send prices higher.

That same mentality dominates the game of MONOPOLY, as players are rewarded by greatly increased rental income for risking their capital to monopolize a set of properties (for most property groups in the game, three constitute a monopoly, mirroring the actual Atlantic City "incentive" to build), and auctions and the trading of title deeds help players build their holdings or raise cash.

In effect, adding houses en route to building a hotel on a MONOPOLY property is something like an early twentieth century Atlantic City proprietor build-

Most of Atlantic City's beachfront hotels, such as the Strand (whose evolution is seen in these cards), began as nineteenth century wooden guesthouses and, as the beach broadened and construction modernized, replaced or joined them with much larger buildings of brick and concrete. The innovative "reinforced concrete" developed by Edison Cement, for example, was first used to construct the Blenheim in 1906. The natural phenomenon of beach expansion due to the buildup of sand (the reverse of what we often see today) posed a quandary to the courts when companies that had sold the land to the hoteliers sued to recover nature's bounty beyond the original "line of storm tide." A legal compromise granted the city waterfront rights between the "high and low water marks," and made the Boardwalk possible.

Hotel Strand at Pennsylvania Ave. and the Beach, Atlantic City, N. J.

77077

ing new wings onto a guest cottage and, eventually, transforming it into a modern hotel. Upkeep, though—in the game as well as on the beachfront—can be costly. Chance and Community Chest cards requiring that a player pay for "repairs" can knock you for a financial loop, since the amount you pay is based on not only how many properties you own, but how much you've built on each one. It can be enough to drop a fat cat from the penthouse to the basement.

Go to Jail

Atlantic City got rolling before a jail was built, and the first prisoners found themselves handcuffed to trees in the mayor's front yard, giving hizzoner a nice view of the common man. This was during the summer; a jailhouse was built the following winter.

Summertime law enforcement had other oddities. It's difficult to fathom today, but less than a century ago, beach attire regulations kept the Atlantic City calendar stuck on January. Bathers wore woolen suits, canvas shoes, straw hats. Women without stockings were not permitted on the beach. It took the Jazz Age in full swing to cue ladies to peel off their leggings. Still, men remained shirted until 1940.

Inland, many lost their shirts in the city's numerous gambling dens, and skin was the currency of choice at the town brothels. Law enforcement was, to be char-itable, inconsistent. Occasional raids netted headlines and, during World War II, Mayor Tommy "Two Guns" Taggart sought to clean up the town in deference to the occupying U.S. Army. But the abiding irony was that, while the Epidermis Police kept the beach skintight, easy virtue proliferated where the sun didn't shine. Atlantic City was rife with the con, the flimflam, pickpockets, bootlegged liquor, numbers runners, and shady characters who had been elbowed out of Philadelphia. In short, disposable cash found a ready home, and a fool and his money were easily parted.

All bets were off because the Atlantic City power structure ran the town like a giant casino long before gambling was legalized. At the top of the political heap was town boss Enoch "Nucky" Johnson, lionized to this day by people who say he took care of the common man as well as himself and his minions. Sure, Atlantic City had a jail, but that was for really bad guys. The scent of sin, of illegality, of freewheeling pleasures not available in the button-down world were what made Atlantic City special.

Taking in the Sights at Atlantic City.

Armed with tape measures, beach "censors" prowled the Atlantic City sands in search of those who would flout city dress regulations. Skirts and trunks were to be within a few inches of the knee, and skin in general was not looked upon favorably. Offenders received summonses for their improprieties. Here a police officer corrals two young ladies whose hemlines may have wandered too far above the knee.

One interpretation of this postcard is that the demure, bookish young lady on the left has a naughtier flipside to her personality (at right). Atlantic City indeed was the perfect spot for such transformations.

In MONOPOLY, jail time is always a threat to disrupt a player's momentum and diminish his bank account. If you land on the "Go to Jail" space or draw a "Go to Jail" card from the Chance or Community Chest decks, you go straight to the clink from any point on the board (no collecting $200 for passing "Go") and you must wait at least until your next turn to get out. Your freedom will likely cost you $50.

Even capitalists must cool their heels when they run afoul of the law. (And smart players know when to stay put for a few turns.)

The Blenheim Hotel assumes Dali-esque contours in this nighttime scene marked by revelry, law enforcement, and a naughty moon.

IN MAY 1899, the Pleasantville and Atlantic City Turnpike Company set a toll charge for the passage of a "horseless carriage" into the resort. Many more tolls and horseless carriages would follow.

After World War II and into the 1950s, the automobile took over in earnest, displacing the train as the prime means of ushering daytrippers and weekenders into Atlantic City. Down the Black Horse and White Horse Pikes (and later, the Atlantic City Expressway) from Philadelphia they came, their passengers rolling down windows to inhale the sour clammy scent of the marshes, poised for that first glimpse of the Atlantic City skyline beyond the reeds.

Atlantic City was well versed in the rules of attraction, and free parking was on the long list of enticements. If cars could park for free, many lawbreakers and nefarious types also could get a free pass in Atlantic City. Under the benevolent despotism of political boss "Nucky" Johnson, the town allowed the rackets to flourish, gave underworld figures the red-carpet treatment, and lapped up bootlegged liquor.

The apotheosis of Atlantic City's dubious pact came in the form of a crime lord conclave in May 1929. Organized-crime leaders from every major city gathered to loll in the surf and talk business. Atlantic City was, after all, a convention town and, for years to come, it remained neutral turf for gangland, which enjoyed the freedom from harassment and kept hands off the local rackets.

During Prohibition, spirits were buoyed by booze courtesy of rumrunners who sped past the Coast Guard and darted into town by ocean or bay. Wealthier customers kept their homes well stocked, as did night spots such as the 500 Club, the Bath and Turf Club, the Hialeah Club, the Clicquot Club, and Babette's, all of which had plenty of gambling on tap as well. Society figures joined street-wise players in the backrooms. Infrequent raids caused proprietors to shuffle the deck but failed to shut them down.

Halfway around the MONOPOLY game board, Free Parking (a public park in MONOPOLY predecessor The Landlord's Game) is a place of rest where players can take stock before jumping back into the fray. That pause can also bring a payoff. A favorite house rule that permits cash payments mandated by Chance and Community Chest for taxes and other bills, as well as other monies held by the "Bank," can enrich the player who lands there, but can also make game play much longer.

CLICQUOT CLUB,
15 North Illinois Avenue,
Atlantic City, N. J.

Above: Bulbous 1940s automobiles fill the lot at Hackney's restaurant. Hotels, restaurants, and night clubs did not want to deter any business, so cars could park for free.
Below: Owner Dan Stebbins changed the name of the Golden Inn at Mississippi and Pacific Avenues to Babette's in 1927, after his new wife's stage name. From the 1920s to the 1940s, the club was busy with backroom gambling and lubricated mingling at its rather elegant yacht bar. Elsewhere in the establishment, a trapdoor led to the roof and a descending stairway for quick getaways.

Above: GOP political boss and Atlantic County Treasurer Enoch L. "Nucky" Johnson was indisputably Atlantic City's master of ceremonies in the '20s and '30s. Comfortable with both gangsters and politicos, he presided over local rackets and rituals with equal aplomb. Here, an unidentified man (left) joins Al Capone (center) and Johnson for a Boardwalk stroll during the four-day "mobsters convention" in May 1929. Nucky booked a number of Jewish gangsters at his headquarters Ritz-Carlton after they had been spurned by another hotel. In 1939, the feds got Nucky (as they had Capone) on income tax evasion. He served four years of a ten-year sentence and returned to a changed Atlantic City.

Opposite, left: The Clicquot Club was one of Atlantic City's prime night spots during an era when street-front night clubs ruled the town's entertainment scene. Along with the 500 Club, the Paradise, and Club Harlem, the Clicquot offered prominent stage shows and hidden gambling, and made both available to underworld figures.

BABETTE'S — MISSISSIPPI AND PACIFIC AVENUES. ATLANTIC CITY, N. J.

BABS

FAMOUS YACHT BAR AND COCKTAIL LOUNGE   ADJOINING OUR DINING ROOM   SEATING 400   61951

PASSING GO

HISTORY HAS CAUGHT UP with the game of MONOPOLY. The year 2005 marks both the centennial of Lizzie Magie's patent for her precursor, The Landlord's Game, and the sesquicentennial of Atlantic City. In the modern global marketplace, MONOPOLY has spawned international editions and other board games steeped in finance and economics. The genial image of Mr. MONOPOLY now pops up on TV commercials, T-shirts, and cereal boxes.

The modern game of MONOPOLY was born of the Depression. Today's game still offers a primer on dollars and cents in a swiftly changing world. Not to mention an exciting journey around the board. To get anywhere in life, you still have to pass Go.

Picture Credits

All the images in this book are from The Collection of Rod Kennedy, Jr., except as noted below:

Courtsey of Ralph Anspach: 8 left

The Atlantic County Historical Society: 36 top left, 60 bottom

Cathy Burke/Irish Pub: 39

The Forbes Collection, New York: 12 top & bottom, 25

Henry George Institute: 9 top & bottom

Hess Photography/Sid Shrier: 87

The Collection of Vicki Gold Levi: 10 left, 13 right, 15 bottom, 28 bottom, 44 top, 62 top, 72 bottom, 76 bottom, 77 bottom, 83 bottom, 93 top left

The West Jersey Chapter of the National

Railway Historical Society: 19 bottom (all Three), 21

New Jersey State Archives: 16 left

Parker Brothers—Hasbro: 11

The Collection of Allen "Boo" Pergament: 18, 29 top, 33 bottom

The Collection of Princeton Antiques & Books: 15 top, 16 right, 17 top & bottom, 19 right, 23 right, 86 bottom

www.uspto.gov: 8 right, 10 right

BACK COVER

Mary Martin, Ltd., Postcards

Bibliography

Anspach, Ralph. *The Billion Dollar MONOPOLY Swindle.* Redwood City, Calif.: Xlibris Corporation, 2000.

Brady, Maxine. *The MONOPOLY Book: Strategy and Tactics of the World's Most Popular Game.* New York: David Mckay Company, 1974.

Butler, Frank. *Book of the Boardwalk and the Atlantic City Story.* Atlantic City: Atlantic City Board of Education, 1952.

Coxey, William J., Frank C. Kozempel, and James E. Kranefeld. *The Trains to America's Playground.* Oaklyn, N. J.: The West Jersey Chapter of the National Railway Historical Society, 1988.

D'Amato, Grace Anselmo. *Chance of a Lifetime.* Harvey Cedars, N. J.: Down The Shore Publishing, 2001.

Ewing, Sarah W. R. *The History of Atlantic City Friends 1856–1966.* Atlantic City, New Jersey: Atlantic City Monthly Meeting of the Religious Society of Friends, 1966.

Funnell, Charles E. *By the Beautiful Sea: The Rise and Hard Times of That Great American Resort, Atlantic City.* New Brunswick, N. J.: Rutgers University Press, 1983.

George, Henry. *Progress and Poverty.* New York: D. Appleton, 1880.

Hapgood, David. *"The Tax to End All Taxes,"* American Heritage Publishing Company, 1978.

Kent, Bill, Robert E. Ruffalo Jr., and Lauralee Dobbins. *Atlantic City: America's Playground.* Encinitas, Calif.: Heritage Media, 1998.

Levi, Vicki Gold, Lee Eisenberg, Rod Kennedy, Jr., and Susan Subtle Dintenfass. *Atlantic City: 125 Years of Ocean Madness.* Berkeley, Calif: Ten Speed Press, 1979.

McMahon, William. *So Young . . . So Gay!* Atlantic City: Atlantic City Press, 1970.

Orbanes, Philip. *The MONOPOLY Companion: The Player's Guide.* Holbrook, Mass.: Adams Media Corporation, 1999.

Reps, John W. *The Forgotten Frontier: Urban planning in the American West Before 1890.* Columbia: University of Missouri Press, 1981.

Waltzer, Jim and Tom Wilk. *Tales of South Jersey: Profiles and Personalities.* New Brunswick, N. J.: Rutgers University Press, 2001.

Index